*Forthcoming Volumes in the New
Church's Teaching Series*

The Anglican Vision
James E. Griffiss

Opening the Bible
Roger Ferlo

Engaging the Word
Michael Johnston

The Practice of Prayer
Margaret Guenther

Living with History
Fredrica Harris Thompsett

Early Christian Traditions
Rebecca Lyman

Opening the Prayer Book
Jeffrey Lee

Mysteries of Faith
Mark McIntosh

Ethics After Easter
Stephen Holmgren

The Christian Social Witness
Harold Lewis

Horizons of Mission
Titus L. Presler

A Theology of Worship
Louis Weil

Christian Wholeness
Martin L. Smith, SSJE

Opening the Prayer Book

The New
Church's Teaching Series,
Volume 7

Opening
the
Prayer Book

Jeffrey Lee

COWLEY PUBLICATIONS
Cambridge • Boston
Massachusetts

The title *The Church's Teaching Series* is used by permission of the Domestic and Foreign Missionary Society. Use of the series title does not constitute the Society's endorsement of the content of the work.

Published in the United States of America by Cowley Publications, a division of the Society of St. John the Evangelist. No portion of this book may be reproduced, stored in or introduced into a retrieval system, or transmitted, in any form or by any means—including photocopying—without the prior written permission of Cowley Publications, except in the case of brief quotations embodied in critical articles and reviews.

Library of Congress Cataloging-in-Publication Data:
Lee, Jeffrey D., 1957–
Opening the prayer book / Jeffrey D. Lee.
p.   cm.   (The new church's teaching series; v. 7)
Includes bibliographical references.
ISBN 1-56101-166-5 (alk. paper)
1. Episcopal Church. Book of common prayer (1790). 2. Episcopal Church—Liturgy. I. Title. II. Series.
BX5945.L45   1999
264'.03—dc21   99-34805
                                                    CIP

Cynthia Shattuck and Vicki Black, editors
Cover design by Vicki Black

This book was printed in Canada by Transcontinental Printing on recycled, acid-free paper.

Second printing

Cowley Publications
28 Temple Place • Boston, Massachusetts 02111
800-225-1534 • www.cowley.org

Table of Contents

The New Church's Teaching Series

Almost fifty years ago a series for the Episcopal Church called The Church's Teaching was launched with the publication of Robert Dentan's *The Holy Scriptures* in 1949. Again in the 1970s the church commissioned another church's teaching series for the next generation of Anglicans. Originally the series was part of an effort to give the growing postwar churches a sense of Anglican identity: what Anglicans share with the larger Christian community and what makes them distinctive within it. During that seemingly more tranquil era it may have been easier to reach a consensus and to speak authoritatively. Now, at the end of the twentieth century, consensus and authority are more difficult; there is considerably more diversity of belief and practice within the churches today, and more people than ever who have never been introduced to the church at all.

The books in this new teaching series for the Episcopal Church attempt to encourage and respond to the times and to the challenges that will usher out the old century and bring in the new. This new series differs from the previous two in significant ways: it has no official status, claims no special authority, speaks in a personal voice, and comes not out of committees but from scholars and pastors meeting and talking informally together. It assumes a different readership: adults who are not "cradle Anglicans," but who come from other religious traditions or from no tradition at all, and who want to know what Anglicanism has to offer.

As the series editor I want to thank E. Allen Kelley, former president of Morehouse Publishing, for initially inviting me to bring together a group of teachers and pastors who could write with learning and conviction about their faith. I am grateful both to him and to Morehouse for participating in the early development of the series.

Since those initial conversations there have been changes in the series itself, but its basic purpose has remained: to explore the themes of the Christian life through Holy Scripture, historical and contemporary theology, worship, spirituality, and social witness. It is our hope that all readers, Anglicans and otherwise, will find the books an aid in their continuing growth into Christ.

James E. Griffiss
Series Editor

Acknowledgments

A favorite teacher of mine used to remind his students that neither the Bible nor *The Book of Common Prayer* had dropped out of heaven in a Glad bag. Well, neither did anything I have to say about the worship offered by God's people. Everything I know and love about the liturgy has come to me as the gift of other believers. It has been shaped first and foremost by my participation in worship as a member of the assembly of the baptized, and further challenged and reformed by the communities of faith I have served as a presbyter. It has been deeply influenced by the gifts of extraordinary teachers and friends.

I want first to thank the parishioners of St. Christopher's Episcopal Church in River Hills, Wisconsin, whose questions and hunger for Christ have called me to be the best pastor and teacher I know how to be. Together, we have reshaped the experience of worship in the parish and found ourselves reshaped in the process. I also want to give thanks to the members of Holy Family Church in Fishers, Indiana. I will always be grateful for their grace and commitment as we established patterns of worship from the ground up.

Particular thanks go to the deacons of the Diocese of Northern Indiana, where I once taught much of this material in the School for Faith and Ministry. The deacons of the church have taught me a great deal about the connections between prayer and action. I believe one of the ministries of the modern diaconate is to teach the presbyters of the church about the nature of priesthood—deacons have been my teachers, at any rate.

Along with many others, I count Louis Weil as one of the most significant influences in my formation as a priest and an adult Christian. His astonishing gift for communicating a passion for the liturgy continues to give life to my own ministry, and my deepest convictions about the church's worship were formed by his teaching.

In preparing this book I owe a debt of gratitude to the generosity of colleagues and friends for their careful reading, comments, and critiques. I am thankful to Ormonde Plater and Leonel Mitchell for helping me spot egregious errors, but also for their kind encouragement; to Doug Sparks and Amy McCreath for their thoughtful comments and questions; and to Wendy Sopkovich for offering her fresh perspectives and honest feedback.

Vicki Black of Cowley Publications knew that this volume needed to be in the series; I am grateful to her, Cynthia Shattuck, and James Griffiss for believing that I might have something of value to contribute and for their searching questions and suggestions. In meetings in Evanston and Boston, via email and over the telephone, the task of editing this book was a rewarding one and an opportunity to relearn many of the things I hold most dear.

Finally, I want to thank my wife Lisa and my children Jonathan and Katherine for their love, support, and understanding of the time a project like this takes, on top of the already overburdened schedule of a parish priest. They are the people in my life who really understand the liturgy.

This book is dedicated to the memory of my mother, who died while it was in its earliest stages. I can still hear her Amens.

Chapter 1

What is Common Prayer?

I recently made a pilgrimage to Nicaragua, and while there I attended the opening liturgy of the annual convention of the Episcopal Diocese of Nicaragua. Apart from the fact that the words of the service were in Spanish, I had the odd feeling that I could have been in any Episcopal parish in North America. Even the tunes of the hymns accompanied by the organ would have been familiar to most regular churchgoers in the United States or Canada, or Great Britain for that matter.

The form of this eucharist was, in fact, the standard Rite II Holy Eucharist from the 1979 *Book of Common Prayer*, in its Spanish version. The congregation was small, and every worshiper had a red prayer book open to the correct page, following the words of the liturgy carefully. After the reading of the lessons and the sermon the page number for the creed was duly announced and everyone turned to it as instructed. Likewise, the page for the prayers of the people, for the eucharistic prayer, the prayer after communion, and so forth. The words of the entire celebration were not only said by the bishop, deacon, and other ministers, they were *read* by the whole congregation.

By contrast, the next evening I attended the eucharist at a cultural center in a poor barrio of Managua. The cultural center is the property of a Roman Catholic Dominican Order whose mission is largely to the children and youth of this barrio. Music lessons are a very popular offering, along with job training classes and a new library. The mass began with half an hour of music, led by twenty or thirty teenagers playing marimbas, recorders, and guitars. There was a song sheet with words to most of the songs printed on it, but only the other visitors like myself seemed to need it. Most people appeared to be singing from memory.

After the singing, the priest who was presiding at this liturgy stood up from where he had been sitting, put on a vestment, and began the opening prayer. There were very few written texts throughout the celebration, certainly none that were put into the hands of worshipers. For the general intercessions, the priest simply pointed to members of the congregation who indicated they had petitions to offer. They announced their concerns one by one and after each the priest invited the assembly to pray. I was told by my Spanish-speaking friend that the eucharistic prayer was largely extemporaneous, although "based on the missal."

I tell this story to illustrate how true it is that Anglicans are people of a book. The words and forms of *The Book of Common Prayer* define our corporate identity perhaps to a degree not true of any other churches—even those with strong liturgical traditions. And not only are the words important for us, the book itself has a tremendous influence on our sense of who we are. There was a time when many, if not most, church members had their own personal copies of the prayer book and brought them to use in church on Sunday mornings. Leather-bound prayer books that belonged to parents or grandparents are still passed down as treasured heirlooms; my father-in-law's combination prayer book and hymnal sits in an honored place on a bookshelf in our house today. I "discovered" the Episcopal Church as a teenager, and one of the first things I did after attending services for a couple of Sundays was to go out and buy my own copy of *The Book of Common Prayer.* I bought the deluxe edition in leather; the paper was the same kind used for Bibles, and the edges of the pages were gold. It felt like a holy object. I did not exactly know how to use it, but I remember paging through the services and lingering over phrases that I heard on Sunday mornings.

Walk into almost any Episcopal Church on a Sunday morning and you will most likely find a congregation worshiping according to *The Book of Common Prayer.* You will also probably see some individual members of the congregation holding copies of the prayer book as they worship. In the backs of pews the prayer books sit next to hymnals. They may not be bound in leather, but the covers might well be red in color and stamped with gold crosses. When a worshiper enters the pew he or she will likely pick up the book and follow the texts printed there as the service unfolds. There will be other books used in the service: the hymnal, perhaps a service leaflet or bulletin, a Bible or a book containing the passages of the Bible to be read that day, and a book on the altar from which the priest reads the prayer over the bread and wine and other parts of the service. Those other books may look important, but it is difficult to escape the conclusion that the most important book in the church is *The Book of Common Prayer.* Episcopalians hold that the Bible "contains all things necessary for salvation," but the book we *use* the most is *The Book of Common Prayer.*

∾ What is Common Prayer?

In Nicaragua I was struck powerfully by the contrast between a Roman Catholic community that felt quite free to adapt the "official" liturgy to its particular setting and situation and an Anglican community that chose to pray the liturgy exactly as the words were printed in the prayer book. One understanding of "common prayer" is simply reciting the words of the prayer book exactly as they are printed on the page. And yet, with the range of options and choices it offers, the 1979 *Book of Common Prayer* was intended to provide greater flexibility and freedom to adapt the liturgy to the concerns and situations of local congregations. It was designed to be more a resource for the creation of local liturgical celebrations than an invariable text that must be used in exactly the same way in every place. Clearly, although our current prayer book has been in use for over twenty years, we are still in the process of understanding what having a book of "common prayer" means.

Although you will find the same prayer book in just about any Episcopal Church you attend today, how the services contained in those books are actually celebrated will vary enormously. The architecture of the church building, the style of music, the number of ordained and lay ministers involved, elaborate or simple ceremonial—processions, bowings, vestments, and so forth—all may be quite different in different congregations. In addition, the 1979 prayer book contains various options for conducting a given service of worship in traditional or contemporary language, for the texts of prayers to be used, and for the way elements of a service are structured. And in future years no doubt even more options for prayer book worship will appear. With all these variations in the way congregations use *The Book of Common Prayer*, what does it mean to talk about common prayer at all?

The Episcopal Church I attended as a teenager was rooted firmly in the Anglo-Catholic tradition. In this particular midwestern parish that meant incense was used, most of the prayers were chanted, vestments were worn by all the liturgical ministers, and the main Sunday service was invariably a celebration of the Holy Eucharist. My experience of worship in this parish (and in the two or three neighboring parishes that had similar worship) led me to expect that all Episcopal churches worshiped this way. I remember going off to college and dutifully looking up the nearest Episcopal church in the newspaper for my first Sunday there. The main service time was given, I found the church, and showed up on Sunday morning. It turned out that the principal service in this parish on that day was Morning Prayer. I had never experienced Morning Prayer, and I wondered if I had walked into the wrong church. I began to realize very quickly that there were wide variations in the way Episcopalians used *The Book of Common Prayer.* Usually other newcomers to the Episcopal Church discover this diversity more quickly than I did. One couple who had been attending the parish I now serve for just a few months took a business trip to another city. On Sunday they went to the nearest Episcopal Church and when they came home the next week they told me, "We didn't even think we were in the same church. Why was it so different?"

Their question does not have an easy answer; in fact, it leads to other fundamental questions about worship in Anglican churches. How can worship look and feel so different in different congregations that are all using the same prayer book and claiming to stand in the same tradition? How can there be such diversity of practice within the same church? What does it mean to say we are bound to each other by common prayer? And what does all this diversity of practice mean about how we understand ourselves to be church? These are important, even central questions to the health and growth of the Episcopal Church and the worldwide Anglican Communion as we face the future.

❧ A Way of Being Church

What exactly is *The Book of Common Prayer?* This question is vitally important to Anglicans because, as we will see, the prayer book's history has been the history of our self-understanding. In this book I want to suggest some answers to the questions of what the prayer book is and what it can be. *The Book of Common Prayer* is far more than the words between the covers of the book. Its texts and directions for ordering worship point to a living tradition, to a distinct way of being Christian. The prayer book has been revised repeatedly over the course of its history—mostly modest revisions until those of the last twenty years or so—but in every revision there are principles, values, and theological perspectives that mark the identity of Anglican corporate prayer.

The Episcopal Church has often been described as a "pragmatic" church. In contrast to confessional churches, in which membership is marked by subscribing in some way to certain doctrinal statements, or to evangelical or Pentecostal churches in which a particular religious experience is expected, Anglicanism offers a practice of common worship. Participation in worship according to *The Book of Common Prayer* historically has marked the boundaries of belonging in this church. The prayer book does not offer precise doctrinal formulations that must be adhered to; rather, it provides the forms that outline our practice of the Christian faith, shaped principally by worship. If you ask an Anglican what it means to belong to the church, the answer might well be, "Come and worship with us." Being an Anglican means doing what the church does—and what the church does, first and foremost, is worship the living God. It is out of our common worship that our understanding of God proceeds and our ethical and moral decision-making takes shape.

A phrase attributed to the fifth-century theologian Prosper of Aquitaine is often quoted by Anglican liturgists: *lex orandi, lex credendi*, the law of prayer establishes the law of belief. The way we pray shapes what we believe. That principle is so important to Anglicanism that any revision of the prayer book causes deep concern and sometimes consternation for members of the church. Virtually every revision of the prayer book has been met with objections and accusations that the faith of the church was being changed. Objections are raised today that the 1979 prayer book represents a wholesale change in the faith and practice of classic Anglicanism—even that it represents a departure from orthodox Christianity. Such anxieties may have to do with a natural resistance to change of any kind, but they may also have to do with underlying theological issues. The change from the language and "feel" of past prayer books to the ethos of the present revision is substantial.

Think, for instance, of the sentence in what is commonly called the Prayer of Humble Access that has appeared in various forms of the eucharist in every *Book of Common Prayer*, including the 1979 prayer book: "We are not worthy so much as to gather up the crumbs under thy Table" (BCP 337). Compare that sentence with one found in Eucharistic Prayer B in our Rite II eucharist: "In him, you have delivered us from evil, and made us worthy to stand before you" (BCP 368). To say the least, these prayers appear to be saying very different things about human beings and about God. And in fact, they express different convictions about our relationship to God that can both be found deep in the scriptures and in the Christian theological tradition.

For centuries, however, only the first perspective—that of our unworthiness—was emphasized in the public prayer of the Anglican Church. The second example—the assurance of our worthiness in Christ to stand before God—is a recovery of a strand of public prayer that was typical in a much earlier age. To say that its inclusion in *The Book of Common Prayer* amounts to a departure from Anglican tradition is to suggest that Anglicanism is not part of the whole sweep of the history of how Christians understood their prayer to express something about their relationship to God. Members of the Church of England in the seventeenth century may not have understood themselves to be worthy in Christ to stand before God, but Christians praying in the third century did: Eucharistic Prayer B is based in part on a eucharistic prayer used in the city of Rome at that time.

～ Varieties of Common Prayer

Contemporary changes to the prayer book such as the inclusion of prayers from the early church have been made in response to the work of international and ecumenical scholars of the Liturgical Movement, the twentieth-century explosion of scholarly inquiry into the worship of the early church and its implications for contemporary life. Their insights led to a revised *Book of Common Prayer* for the Episcopal Church, with more variety and liturgical options than any previous book. And what is true for the prayer book of the Episcopal Church in the United States is also true of the alternative and revised prayer books of other parts of the Anglican Communion, as other Anglican churches have also sought to incorporate the insights of contemporary scholarship and the recovery of ancient forms of worship into their own life of prayer.

For some people the variety is alarming; it means an end to the assumption that you could walk into an Anglican church anywhere in the world and hear the same service. On the surface, that fear is well-founded: the words are no longer the same in every place. Does that mean then that Anglicans can no longer share a common faith, a common way of being church? It does not. The revision of Anglican prayer books in the twentieth century share profound common insights about the nature of worship and the worshiping community. The revised prayer books are no longer simply clones of the original English version, but are the expression of worship among living communities of Christians in the Anglican tradition. The 1979 *Book of Common Prayer* is just one example among a growing range of revised and alternative prayer books in the Anglican Communion with a "common family resemblance."[1] And not every member of a family has every family characteristic.

When Anglicans talk about "common prayer" we do not mean that every worshiping congregation is doing exactly the same thing in exactly the same way. Although it is true that for most of our history the words of the spoken texts have been more or less the same in every congregation, rarely would they have been assembled in precisely the same way or accompanied by the same gestures, ornaments, or music. In the sixteenth century, for example, various requirements governed the use of different kinds of vestments in cathedrals, collegiate churches, and parish churches. The music of the liturgy in the chapel of

Elizabeth I was considerably more elaborate than the simple musical settings provided for parish churches of the time. At times in the seventeenth century altars were placed against the east wall of churches and were fenced in by altar rails; at other times, they were standing freely in the middle of chancels. The revival of interest in medieval liturgy and ceremonial in the nineteenth century meant that in some churches the Sunday service looked like a fourteenth-century solemn high mass, while others used the same prayer book to celebrate a simple service of Morning Prayer and sermon. In short, among Anglicans common prayer has always looked and felt different in different places. The differences have become more obvious to us today for a variety of reasons: the variations the current prayer books encourage in the texts themselves, our ability to travel, and the awareness of differences made obvious by media coverage.

You will find that I spend a good deal of time in this book tracing the history of the development of liturgy. My purpose in doing so is to show the wide diversity of Christian worship from its beginnings. Liturgical variation is not simply a modern phenomenon; in fact, the notion that the liturgy should or could be celebrated the same way in every place was a long time in coming. Yet because of the unique circumstances of the Reformation in England, Anglicans are the inheritors of a pattern of liturgical uniformity established by law. The 1979 *Book of Common Prayer,* with its variations and options, represents a significant challenge to the ideal of uniformity of worship.

One of the challenges facing Anglicanism worldwide is the increasing diversity of its prayer books; *A*

New Zealand Prayer Book, for example, bears very little resemblance to the established prayer book of the Church of England. The words of a Roman Catholic liturgical scholar, reflecting on the diversity of liturgical practice in earlier ages, bear repeating here:

> This information...should serve to comfort all those who are shocked by the fact that...the centuries-old, cast-iron uniformity of liturgical books and prayers has been abandoned in favour of an attempt to make the liturgy correspond more closely to the needs of different people and different countries. For surely, if the Church was able to tolerate variations in the liturgy even within the one city of Rome and moreover was not ashamed of this, then in the same way she will also be able to tolerate the fact that in the future the liturgy will only be universally the same in respect of its fundamental principles, but will differ widely as to the manner in which it is put into practice.[2]

So common prayer does not mean absolute uniformity and almost never has; it means something else, something deeper. It points to a shared life, a common stance toward the mystery of God. It represents a way of believing, a methodology if you will for practicing the Christian faith.

～ Revising Our Common Prayer

A priest I know tells this story of two members in his congregation. Around the time when the 1979 prayer book was being introduced, one parishioner who was devoted to the 1928 prayer book withdrew his pledge and effectively left the parish with a flurry of angry letters to the rector. A friend of his, another man the rector knew to be unhappy with the "new" book, made an appointment to see him. The rector braced himself for another angry departure. But when the man came to see him he said, "Father, you know I don't like this new prayer book." His rector assured him that he did know that. "And you know Fred has left the parish and taken his pledge with him." The rector said he did indeed know that too. "Well," said the man, "I may not like this book, but I'm here to pay my pledge and Fred's too. While I'll never be happy with this prayer book, we're family."

When I was a young priest in my first parish, I was asked to visit a number of homebound parishioners. One lady who was well into her nineties always welcomed my visits, and I enjoyed bringing Holy Communion to her. She had not been able to be in church for many years, so—priding myself on my pastoral sensitivity—I prepared a service leaflet for the home communion in language from the 1928 prayer book. We used that service for several months until one afternoon my friend asked me almost sheepishly about the words on the leaflet. "Are these the prayers they're using in church these days?" she asked. "Well, no," I said, and explained about the new prayer book. "That's what I thought," she said. "Do you think we could use what you're using on Sunday morning? I don't speak Elizabethan . . . do you? I don't want to be out of touch with the life of my church."

The Book of Common Prayer provides an environment in which the ancient faith of Christians can continually find new expression in the lives of living members of Christ's body. The words of the prayer book are subject to change and indeed have been revised from time to time. One of the principles of the Reformation was that worship should be in a language the people could understand. The current prayer book is one of the latest attempts to render the words of our worship in the language people use. But the language of worship encompasses much more than the spoken word. It includes objects that communicate wordlessly but with great power: water, oil, bread, wine, the touch of a human hand. Movement, gesture, art, and music all communicate too, and the meaning of these nonverbal languages shifts with time just as much as the words themselves. The words and forms of our worship can be assembled in a variety of ways for a variety of purposes, but taken together, they outline a pattern for the life of Christian people in the church as they live out their lives in this world. Revision is necessary from time to time if that pattern is to remain alive.

In short, *The Book of Common Prayer* is not simply a religious artifact in a museum of antique religious languages. It is not merely an example of poetic literature expressing holy thoughts about God. It is fundamentally a tool, and as with any tool, the people who use it determine the effect it will have. The prayer book can be used skillfully with satisfying and beautiful results, or it can be handled clumsily, with less desirable results. I have a friend who collects antique woodworking tools. The first time I visited his workshop I was stunned to see these rare and expensive tools lying on the workbench. "You use these?" I asked. "Of course," came the reply. "Why else have them? But you have to know what you're doing." The people who use the prayer book will shape the liturgies within it according to their skill, knowledge, and beliefs, and the resulting liturgies will reflect the infinite variety of gifts within the church.

How do you use the prayer book? How does your congregation use it? How have other congregations where you may have worshiped used it? Do you know why? These are questions that can be answered in many different ways and at many different levels. First-time visitors to an Episcopal church often register confusion about finding their place in the prayer book, juggling it with hymnals and service leaflets. How to use the prayer book is an important question in helping newcomers to feel welcome.

But even when the order of service is made crystal clear, when it is made as "user-friendly" as possible, there are still questions about what it *means* to worship according to a particular liturgical tradition, like that of *The Book of Common Prayer.* Knowing something of the history of the prayer book and the tradition that produced it is essential to understanding the meaning of worshiping in this particular way. Common prayer means that every worshiper is a user of the set of tools called *The Book of Common Prayer.* Every worshiper, therefore, should know what he or she is doing—what the tools are designed to do, where they come from, how their use has changed, and new ways to use them.

ᔦ The Future

The spirituality of Anglicanism is sustained by the living tradition of *The Book of Common Prayer.* That spirituality is rooted firmly in the Christian past and at the same time is open to God's future. It is a spirituality of the Incarnation and of the paschal mystery— the Easter mystery of the death and resurrection of Christ. With Christians of every time and place we gather to remember and proclaim the Lord's death until Christ comes again. We proclaim the death and resurrection of Christ as people who live as the body of Christ in this world. To follow Christ means participating in Christ's death and resurrection: dying to self in order to be raised with Christ. We must find ways to speak of that mystery so it will be understood in our world, even if that means dying to long cherished languages, images, or customs.

The preface to *The Book of Common Prayer* begins with words printed in every American prayer book since 1789:

> It is a most invaluable part of that blessed "liberty wherewith Christ hath made us free," that in his worship different forms and usages may without offence be allowed, provided the substance of the Faith be kept entire; and that, in every Church, what cannot be clearly determined to belong to Doctrine must be referred to Discipline; and therefore, by common consent and authority, may be altered, abridged, enlarged, amended, or otherwise disposed of, as may seem most convenient for the edification of the people, "according to the various exigency of times and occasions." (BCP 9)

As we stand on the verge of the twenty-first century these words are significant. Questions of what pertains to doctrine and discipline are hotly debated in the church, as we seek to discover how Christian people can "speak the meaning of God for our world."[3] Issues of language that does not specify gender, the blessing of same-sex relationships, the adoption of rituals and images from native cultures, the use of contemporary and popular musical idioms—all these questions are making their presence felt in the process of enlarging our repertoire of public prayer. As we engage these questions, I believe we are called to explore the deep structures underlying the prayer book. We need to be anchored in the classic shape of the church's liturgical tradition, so that in our worship we may have a place to stand as we address the gospel to people who have concerns unknown to previous generations. This book is offered as a companion to communities of Christians who want to open up the prayer book and let it speak.

Chapter 2

The Pattern of Prayer

In the gymnasium of a suburban middle school, a group of people gather in as much silence as they can manage, given the presence of a large number of children under the age of eight. A priest and assistant ministers enter the area at one end of the gym that has been arranged for worship and they kneel there before a large table. Everyone joins in kneeling and a fidgety silence is kept. Out of the silence, the priest invites the people to pray and then says these words:

> Almighty God, we pray you graciously to behold this your family, for whom our Lord Jesus Christ was willing to be betrayed, and given into the hands of sinners, and to suffer death upon the cross; who now lives and reigns with you and the Holy Spirit, one God, for ever and ever. Amen.

A new Episcopal church in suburban Indianapolis has just begun to celebrate for the first time the Good Friday liturgy from *The Book of Common Prayer.*

On this day a larger than usual number of first-time visitors have come, and those who have prepared this celebration watch nervously to make sure the newcomers are able to participate. Scripture passages are read. The psalms are chanted to ancient melodies. From John's gospel the story of the crucifixion of Jesus is sung. A sermon is preached. A long series of intercessions follows. After the prayers, a large wooden cross is carried in from outside the doors of the gymnasium; a woman carrying a bowl of burning incense precedes it. While a contemporary song about the cross of Jesus is sung, people get up from their seats and come to touch the wood of the cross; some kneel for a moment, others simply want to be near it. Some of the children bring flowers they have pulled from the yard outside and leave them at the foot of the cross. The service ends simply with the saying of the Lord's Prayer and one additional prayer.

I was the "church planter" for the congregation keeping this Good Friday. Holy Family Episcopal Church had begun officially just a few months earlier with a gathering of twelve people or so in the living room of our home. We grew quickly to the point of needing a large space for worship and the local school made its gym available. From the beginning we worshiped according to a fairly straightforward use of the prayer book. The Sunday eucharist was Rite II, with a few seasonal changes. Our music was from *The Hymnal 1982* and a few supplemental resources that were easier to accompany on our necessarily portable instruments of guitar and electronic keyboard.

The congregation was made up in large part of people who were previously unchurched or who had come from other religious traditions. Some had not been active in any church for a long time. We took great care to make the prayer book liturgy as accessible to these newcomers as possible—a particular challenge for the rites of Holy Week. We intended to celebrate the services of Maundy Thursday, Good Friday, and the Great Vigil of Easter as richly as our resources allowed, although we wondered how these rather elaborate, symbolically rich celebrations would strike people in the congregation.

One couple in particular I had just met the previous week had me worried. They had attended one Sunday service and I had invited them to join in the observance of Thursday, Friday, and Saturday night. Had I made a mistake? Like so many other people in this fast-growing, upwardly mobile suburb, they had been looking for a church for a while, shopping around for one that would best "meet their needs." They and others like them were the reason we tried to make the prayer book services easy to use.

As it turned out, I did not need to worry about this man and woman at all. After the service that day, they came up to me as we were leaving the gym. They were moved; they were elated. I had seen them come to the cross and watched as they stayed there while others came up to it and went. "This is it," they said. "This is exactly what we've been looking for and did not know how to ask for it—something older than what the pastor thought up last week."

～ Things Old and New

The Book of Common Prayer stands as a contemporary expression of an ancient tradition. Indeed, the order I

have described for the celebration of Good Friday in
the 1979 *Book of Common Prayer* contains elements
that can be traced from medieval Sarum rites celebrated in England back to the pilgrim Egeria's description of the Good Friday liturgy as it was celebrated in
the fourth century by the church in Jerusalem.
Likewise, the opening prayer of the service quoted
above dates from another early medieval document,
called the Gregorian sacramentary, that was compiled
in the late eighth century.[1] This reliance on ancient
patterns and texts could easily lead to a certain kind
of antiquarianism, a fascination with recreating worship exactly as it was done in the twelfth or fourth or
nineteenth centuries. Anglicanism has been accused—
sometimes justly—of an obsession with the preservation of historical or cultural forms for their own sake.
But there is a distinction to be made between *tradi-
tionalism* and *tradition*. Jaroslav Pelikan put it well:
"Tradition is the living faith of the dead; traditional-
ism is the dead faith of the living."[2] What one young
couple discovered on that Good Friday, I trust, was a
community worshiping and being formed in faith by
a living tradition.

The traditional pattern of Christian worship is
rooted deeply in the Bible itself. It is not just that
Christian worship gives a central role to the reading of
passages of scripture. The members of the church
gather to do what scripture itself does: to speak a new
word of God's presence and grace in the words of
those who have experienced that presence in the past.
It is what the prophet Isaiah does when he speaks to
the people of Israel who have been taken into exile. He
tells them to forget the old story of the Exodus from

Egypt, even while he relies on its imagery to announce that God is about to do a brand new thing for them (Isaiah 43:18ff).

It is also what Jesus does on the night before he meets with death. He takes the Jewish tradition of the ritual fellowship meal with its long-established blessing of bread and cup and fills it with the new meaning of his own life and death (Matthew 26:26ff). The liturgical scholar Gordon Lathrop calls this characteristic of Christian worship a basic pattern of "juxtaposition." In other words, we place the record of the experience of God's action in the past alongside our current needs, longings, and experiences and in doing so cause a new reality to come into being.

> Christian corporate worship is biblical . . . in much of the way it uses texts and understands them to be meaningful. That use is complex. The texts are not simply read, as in a lecture hall or even a theater. They are received with reverence, yet they are criticized and transformed. They become the environment for the encounter with God and with God's grace. They become language for current singing.[3]

When we hear the words of scripture and pray the words of the liturgy, we are placing them alongside the memories, events, and hopes of our lives. In this way our worship both recreates us and is recreated by us.

I remember a breakfast meeting I had with a young man who had attended the eucharist in our parish just a couple of times. He wanted to explore membership in the Episcopal Church on the basis of what he had experienced in the liturgy. He told me he had grown up in a non-liturgical tradition and was exhilarated by what he experienced in worship with us. What was it that he found so attractive, I wanted to know. "You don't try and explain everything," he said. "You let the words and the symbols be there so they can belong to everybody. That was more meaningful to me than all the explanations of the Bible I've ever gotten—because it's always somebody else's explanation."

To stand in a living tradition of worship is to know that ancient texts and ritual patterns can be made to speak new realities and thus be transformed. It is *our* lives that we bring when we assemble to be God's people and hear the story of the saving of Israel, and the Exodus must become *our* liberation. It is our bread and wine, our eating and drinking, but both are given new meaning by the death and resurrection of Christ.

∾ Worship in the Time of Jesus

I have occasionally been asked by friends of mine in other church traditions, "Why do you Episcopalians maintain all those ceremonies? Prayer books, vestments, processions—why do you need all that? Why can't you just worship like Jesus and the disciples did in the upper room?" Beneath those questions lies a misunderstanding of what is actually portrayed in the biblical accounts of Jesus' meal with his friends. The last supper did not occur in a vacuum; Jesus did not create the prayers said during that meal out of nothing. The act of blessing God for gifts of mercy and deliverance had a particular ritual shape in Judaism. Blessings, or *berakoth*, were made according to traditional patterns of blessing God for saving actions in the past and pleading for that same saving action now. Beyond the words of blessing, the meal itself unfolded according to a definite ritual pattern. Bread and wine were blessed at prescribed moments, and only certain persons could be present for the final solemn prayer.[4] The supposed informality and spontaneity of Jesus' final meal with his disciples was not so simple or so new.

Beyond the question of the character of the last supper and its meaning for the development of the Christian eucharist lies the whole complex of Jewish worship practices at the time of Jesus. At that time there were three centers of Jewish worship: the temple, the synagogue, and the home.[5] The gospels present us with images of the importance of these centers to Jesus as he engaged in worship, and each one exercised a distinctive influence on the worship of the earliest Christians.

The temple was a place of sacrifice. It was to the temple that Jesus' parents brought him as an infant to offer the customary sacrifices after his circumcision (Luke 2:21ff. The temple was also a place of teaching: the twelve-year-old Jesus was found there by his parents, sitting among the teachers, "listening to them and asking them questions" (Luke 2:46ff). It was to the temple that Jesus would return for many of the most dramatic episodes in his public ministry, culminating with his last visit and his directions for celebrating the Passover in Jerusalem (Mark 14:12ff). Jesus was an observant keeper of the temple festivals and a frequent visitor, as were his first disciples and apparently the earliest members of the post-resurrection church in Jerusalem. The language of the temple and its ritual would provide potent images for Christian worship long after Christians had ceased to observe its rites. The early church's understanding of the death and resurrection of Christ was worked out in the writings of the New Testament through the symbolism of the temple and its sacrificial system, as seen so clearly in the letter to the Hebrews and the Revelation to John.

The synagogue, on the other hand, was primarily a place of teaching. Reading and interpreting the scriptures were the main features of synagogue worship, which at the time of Jesus took place regularly on the sabbath and holy days. Jesus is pictured as a regular attender of synagogue services: during his trip to Nazareth he "went to the synagogue on the sabbath day, as was his custom" (Luke 4:16). When the disciples began to carry the good news of Jesus' death and resurrection beyond Jerusalem, they did so by going first to synagogues and making their case in those assemblies. Instruction and initiation of converts took place in the synagogue, a pattern that Christians followed in their emerging practices of initiation during the first three or four centuries.[6] As the earliest churches began to form congregations apart from the synagogue, they gradually moved their principal gathering from the sabbath to the first day of the week, the Lord's Day. Yet it is likely that they continued to model their worship on the service of the synagogue, with the addition of the distinctively Christian elements of the eucharistic meal and the baptismal bath.

Our patterns of personal, daily prayer likewise have their roots in Jewish tradition. In Judaism the

home was the center of personal prayer and the
domestic ritual of daily prayer also had its influence in
the development of Christian worship. Although the
prescribed hours of prayer three times a day were
observed publicly in the synagogue (corresponding to
the hours of sacrifice in the temple), it is not likely
that large numbers of people were able to attend the
daily services.[7] Instead, most devout Jews probably
prayed at the appointed hours privately, along with
the morning and evening recitation of the *Shema*,
"Hear, O Israel, the Lord our God is one." Festive meals
and other family occasions were marked by the recitation of ritual prayers and, in the case of the evening
meal on Fridays and Saturdays, the ceremonial lighting of a lamp to mark the beginning and end of the
sabbath.

Not much can be said with certainty about the earliest Jewish-Christian observance of times of daily
prayer, but elements of domestic and synagogue practice can be identified in the emerging worship patterns
of the early church. Their influence continues even
today. For example, the ritual lamp lighting ceremony, with its blessing of God for the gift of light,
remains a feature of the prayer book's Order of
Worship for the Evening and is at the very heart of the
church's liturgical life in the lighting of the paschal
candle at the Great Vigil of Easter.

~ Early Christian Liturgies
In the first centuries of the life of the church, the
structure of its worship began to take on the distinctive shape we know today. The classic outline of
Christian initiation, the eucharist, and daily prayer

becomes discernible during the first five centuries of the church's life. This pattern has persisted through centuries of liturgical development, although at times it has been obscured or elaborated almost beyond recognition.

In large measure, the story of modern liturgical reform, including the creation of the 1979 *Book of Common Prayer*, can be read as the story of the attempt to recover—or *uncover*—the deep structures of Christian worship that came into being during this early period. Again, while critics have sometimes charged liturgical scholars with a certain kind of antiquarianism, this recovery of early church insights and structures has informed the pastoral challenges and living theological currents of our own time. Clearly, it is pointless to try to recreate worship as it was experienced at some idealized time in the past. On the other hand, it *is* important to ask what insights from the past have something important to say to the mission of the church in our own time.

Before we look at the characteristics of Christian worship in what is called the patristic period (the time of the "church fathers"—the first several hundred years of the church's history), we need first to ask *how* we know what we know about the way Christians worshiped at this time. What original literary material do we have dating from this period? Many of the texts we have contain descriptions of the early church's liturgical celebrations and even, in some cases, the actual texts used. Some of this source material was known before the nineteenth century, but much of it has come to light only since about 1870.

These documents provide different kinds of information about the worship of the early church. Some of the material is descriptive, telling how prayers or liturgies were conducted in particular places and times. An especially significant example of descriptive writing is the *Pilgrimage of Egeria*, the diary of a Spanish nun who visited the Holy Land about the year 400. She describes the worship of the Christian community there in much the same way that today we might report on what we experienced on a visit to Rome or Canterbury. Her descriptions of the lengthy and elaborate rites of what we know as Holy Week and Easter are particularly important. The outline of the major liturgical gatherings she attends—a procession with branches, commemoration of the last supper, gathering to sing the glory of the cross of Christ, the vigil of Easter—is reflected in the outline of the prayer book services we have today.

Other materials were written to defend or explain the practices of Christians. An early and important example of this kind of writing is the *Apology* of Justin Martyr, dated about the year 155. He writes to both Roman and Jewish audiences to defend and explain Christian worship against misunderstandings and rumors. This small excerpt should sound familiar to anyone participating in a eucharist according to *The Book of Common Prayer* today:

> And on the day named after the sun, all who live in city or countryside assemble, and the memoirs of the apostles or the writing of the prophets are read for as long as time allows. When the lector has finished, the president addresses us, admonishing us and exhorting us

to imitate the splendid things we have heard.
Then we all stand and pray, and . . . bread, wine,
and water are brought up. The president offers
prayers of thanksgiving, . . . the gifts over which
thanksgiving has been spoken are distributed,
and each one shares in them, while they are also
sent via the deacons to the absent brethren . . . .
The reason why we all assemble on Sunday is
that it is the first day: the day on which God
transformed darkness and matter and created
the world, and the day on which Jesus Christ
our Savior rose from the dead.[8]

Still other documents provide actual prayer texts
used in early church worship. The earliest example we
have of the text of a complete eucharistic prayer, for
instance, comes from the *Apostolic Tradition* of
Hippolytus of Rome, dated about the year 215. He
records a eucharistic prayer for use at the consecration of a bishop. It begins with a familiar dialogue:

The Lord be with you.
  And with your spirit.
Up with your hearts.
  We have them with the Lord.
Let us give thanks to the Lord.
It is fitting and right.

Then the bishop continues:

We render thanks to you, O God, through your
beloved child Jesus Christ, whom in the last
times you sent to us as saviour and redeemer
and angel of your will; who is your inseparable
Word, through whom you made all things and

in whom you were well pleased. You sent him
from heaven into the Virgin's womb; and, con-
ceived in the womb, he was made flesh and was
manifested as your Son.... Fulfilling your will
and gaining for you a holy people, he stretched
out his hands when he should suffer, that he
might release from suffering those who have
believed in you.[9]

The discovery of documents such as these has rev-
olutionized our understanding of the practice of worship in the early church. We owe much of the impetus
for revision of pastoral and liturgical practice in our
own time to the work of literary and liturgical scholars who have uncovered, reconstructed, and translated them. These ancient texts have led to new insights
about the mission of the worshiping Christian community not just in the ancient world, but in the modern church as well. They have shaped modern
revisions of the liturgy in part because of a growing
realization that the church of our own time faces circumstances more like those of the first few centuries
than those of the middle ages or the post-Reformation
era. Today Christians all over the world find themselves faced increasingly with a hostile or indifferent
culture, rather than one in which their values are
assumed. The liturgical life of the early church arose
in just such circumstances.

∾ Christian Initiation

Those who are persuaded and believe that the
things we teach and say are true, and promise
that they can live accordingly, are instructed to

pray and beseech God with fasting for the remission of their past sins, while we pray and fast along with them. Then they are brought by us where there is water, and are reborn by the same manner of rebirth by which we ourselves were reborn; for they are washed in the water in the name of God the Father and Master of all, and of our Savior Jesus Christ, and of the Holy Spirit.[10]

As the church moved out from its original Jewish setting into the gentile world, its worship practices changed. The first challenge was communicating the story of Jesus in terms that could be understood by those outside the Jewish faith tradition. The first Jewish followers of Christ may have taken the symbols and language of the Hebrew scriptures for granted, but as the church included more and more gentile converts, it could do so no longer. Therefore the primary task of the church of the first, second, and third centuries was to shape its worship—and in particular its initiatory practice—to its new context and self-understanding, while still remaining faithful to its historical foundations. How was it possible to speak of the death, resurrection, and glorification of Jesus, whom Christians believed to be the fulfillment of the hopes and longings of the people of Israel, to Greeks and Romans who knew little or nothing of the story of Passover or the Exodus?

Christians faced a number of pastoral and evangelistic questions in the face of an often hostile or indifferent gentile society. A principal concern of the church was to define itself and to delineate its boundaries. One response to this challenge was the development of a formal period of training, teaching, and probationary membership leading to baptism that came to be known as the catechumenate. The origins of the catechumenate can be identified as early as the first century, and it was fully developed and well-established by the third century. Its importance for the self-understanding of the church as it developed is hard to overstate. The Christian faith as we know it today was shaped in profound ways by the early church's practice of forming new converts through the catechumenate.

Around the turn of the third century Clement of Alexandria wrote a handbook of instruction for newly baptized Christians called the *Paidagogos*. Commenting on this work, theologian Richard Norris describes the seriousness with which Christians of this period took the practice of baptismal discipline and formation:

> The Church is not a religious institution in the service of its society; it is *another* society, living a new and different sort of life, which one enters only through a personal revolution—i.e., a turnabout, a conversion. . . . The Church is "different," and deliberately and necessarily so. But more than that, Clement does not envisage the life of this odd community, as we normally do, in terms of "ministry," but in terms of discipleship.[11]

The church's worship, immersed in the images and language of ancient Israel, found new expression in the lives of these new Christians. Their own personal stories were grafted onto the story of God's saving deeds in Israel in the past, and so became the story of

God's saving deeds in the church, now. In baptism the new Christian passed through the Red Sea to join in the journey of the new people of the covenant. Slavery to sin was broken. God provided food for the journey, a foretaste of the banquet to come.

We know that the Christians of this period experienced baptism as a complex event filled with lavish sacramental signs. Baptism was a journey beginning with evangelization and conversion; the teaching and formation of the catechumenate led to the water bath, anointing with oil, and first communion, and then beyond to *mystagogia*, a period of instruction on the meaning of what the newly baptized person had experienced. While practices varied from place to place, we do know from archeological and literary evidence that the baptismal bath and anointing were experienced as dramatically natural actions: converts were truly bathed. They took off their clothes and were either immersed in water or liberally doused—and thus they experienced a watery rebirth into a new identity. Then they were massaged with oil—an extravagant sign of that new identity as a member of the risen body of Christ, the Anointed One.[12] The radical commitment enacted by this kind of baptismal practice has fueled the imagination and work of many liturgical reformers of our own day.

The shape of baptism was well-established by the end of the third century, although details differed in various places. In its barest outline, the process of initiation involved a period of probationary membership involving training and scrutiny, the water bath, anointing and laying on of hands, and full admission to the eucharistic assembly.

～ The Eucharist

> Thou, Lord, didst make all for thy pleasure,
> didst give us food for all our days,
> giving in Christ the Bread eternal;
> thine is the power, be thine the praise . . . .
>
> As grain, once scattered on the hillsides,
> was in this broken bread made one,
> so from all lands thy Church be gathered
> into thy kingdom by thy Son.[13]

A colleague of mine was recently called to be rector of a new church. Although the vestry had indicated they were willing to redesign the altar area of the church to accommodate a freestanding altar table, when the altar was moved they encountered more resistance from the congregation than anyone ever thought they would. She said, "I realized although they pray about gathering up crumbs under the table every Sunday and their favorite communion hymn is about Christ as living bread, no one really believed that the eucharist was a meal. It was a more like a sacred drama."

The earliest eucharistic meals of Christians were just that: meals. Developing as we have seen from the fellowship meals of Judaism, they were experiences of gathering with the Risen One at table. Early Christians called this meal the "breaking of the bread," and it was filled with the significance of Jesus' death and resurrection. Small groups of Christians would gather in one another's homes on the first day of the week to share this meal, in the course of which the one presiding would bless the bread and the cup, and so obey the

Lord's command to "do this" in his memory.[14] It was a fairly intimate ritual meal, but a meal nonetheless, complete with the passing of dishes and plates—a real feeding of bodily hunger.

Exactly when the eucharistic blessings of bread and cup were removed from the context of the larger meal is unclear, but by the time of Justin Martyr's description of the eucharist around 155 the separation has occurred. He describes a liturgical event with an outline that would be familiar to anyone celebrating the eucharist according to *The Book of Common Prayer.* The congregation gathers to hear readings from the Hebrew scriptures and the "memoirs of the Apostles," a homily is preached, the people stand to offer intercessory prayer, bread and wine are presented to the presider, who says a thanksgiving over these gifts (the prayer is apparently improvised but follows a definite pattern), the people respond "Amen," and the gifts are distributed. Thus, it would seem that by the middle of the second century the eucharist already had the essential shape we know it by today.

It is also in the second and third centuries that the meal first comes to be called *eucharistia* and to be identified by the action at its heart: the presentation of gifts and the giving of thanks. In the eucharist we give thanks for the redemptive death and resurrection of Christ and the assurance that, through the power of the Holy Spirit, our redemption is now a present reality. The emphasis in this period is on the "doing" of the meal: there is little of the speculation about the manner of Christ's presence in the eucharist that would later so dominate the church's approach to the sacrament. Even in the writings of the conservative

Hippolytus of Rome, who became embroiled in theological controversies over the doctrine of the Trinity, we see no evidence of an attempt to define what was taking place in the eucharistic meal. What we do see in his work *Apostolic Tradition* is an insistence on the *pattern* of the eucharistic liturgy and a detailed description of the eucharist in the church at Rome as he knew it. It is interesting that Hippolytus is quite clear about the *way* things are done, but he says explicitly that the *words* of the eucharistic prayer may be made according to the ability of the presider, following an accepted model (an example of which he provides). In other words, the prayer was in the presider's own words, but according to the received pattern.[15] The insistence on fixed formulas of words had not yet taken place.

～ Daily Prayer

Very little is known about the practice of public daily prayer during the first three centuries, except to say that it was taking place. There are scattered references throughout the source documents to indicate that it was important, but little description of the shape or content of that prayer is offered in detail. Nevertheless, here too a pattern begins to emerge, one that would change dramatically over the coming centuries.

We know that the earliest Christians learned about the practice of daily prayer from the synagogue and temple traditions. Public prayer in the morning and evening, supplemented with lesser times of prayer during the course of the day, was the pattern inherited from Judaism and then adapted by Jewish and

gentile Christians. Whether large numbers of
Christians were able to gather daily—and there are
some indications that they did—or whether the times
were observed informally at first, very quickly there
emerged a public celebration of daily prayer.[16]

Presided over by the bishop, who was assisted by
presbyters and deacons, daily prayer was seen to be
the business of the whole church. Prayer in the morning was a celebration of the resurrection of Christ,
while prayer in the evening was the daily remembrance of Christ's death and burial. The shape of these
daily services allowed them to be genuinely popular:
they were the prayers "of the people" because they
were easy to participate in. They included short
psalms and hymns having to do with Christ, acts of
praise, perhaps including often-repeated alleluias or
other acclamations, and intercessions at length.
Ceremonially, these services are thought to have been
rather colorful, with a ritual lighting of lamps and the
offering of incense in the evening, for example. They
did not ordinarily include scripture readings or a sermon since they were considered an offering of worship rather than an opportunity for instruction.

The daily offices of Morning and Evening Prayer in
the 1979 *Book of Common Prayer* are more closely
related to the offices of the later monastic tradition,
which began to emerge in the early middle ages and
were soon characterized by the development of a con-
tinuous reading of scripture and lengthy psalmody. In
practice, however, the prayer book services of choral
Evensong and Sunday Morning Prayer, like the daily
liturgies of the early church, became popular offices in
many places, with elaborate ceremonial and canticles

and psalms people knew by heart. The service known in the 1979 prayer book as An Order of Worship for the Evening represents an attempt to recover the spirit of the earlier popular or "cathedral" office, as it is sometimes called. A notable example of an even more fully developed popular evening office is found in *The Book of Alternative Services* of the Anglican Church of Canada. Called A Vigil of the Resurrection, it is modeled in great detail on the weekly vigil of the early church.

By the end of the fourth century, then, the worship of the Christian people in the west had developed the essential patterns that would remain distinguishing features through a long, complicated, and sometimes contentious history:

- The weekly gathering on the first day of the week, the day of the Lord's resurrection;
- The yearly commemoration of the Christian Passover, the death and resurrection of Christ;
- Initiation as formation, bathing, anointing, and communing of new Christians;
- The eucharistic liturgy of gathering, proclamation of scripture, intercession, offering, giving thanks, eating and drinking; and
- Offices of daily prayer that included praise and intercession in the morning and evening.

This ancient pattern of liturgical celebration is still the basis of our common life of worship. Although its essential features are obscured sometimes by secondary concerns, if you look carefully at *The Book of Common Prayer* you will see this pattern clearly at its heart. The prayer book is certainly "something older than what the pastor thought up last week"; it is part of the way in which God has encountered centuries of Christians with the living presence of Jesus Christ in the power of the Holy Spirit, the way God has acted and continues to act to make the church new.

Chapter 3

The Prayer Book is Born

The year 1999 marks the four hundred fiftieth anniversary of the first *Book of Common Prayer* of 1549. Symposia and lectures, articles and books (like this one!) are being produced to celebrate the prayer book legacy. Some of these celebrations include recreations of historical liturgies according to one or another version of the prayer book. A friend of mine, after attending a service done in fine historical style according to the 1549 prayer book, wrote to me, "It was great. Just like being at the 'Old Vic.'" It may be a helpful educational exercise to participate in an act of worship "just as it was done" in a given historical period. It is tempting to think of the history of Christian worship in this way—like visiting a museum. But my purpose in detailing here the history of the prayer book is to show how the tradition lives, and how, like all living things, it has grown and changed.

In a sense, *The Book of Common Prayer* as a book is a product of the medieval church and its liturgical development. In the earliest days of the church, as we have seen, the liturgy came to be celebrated according to defined patterns, though with great variety both of text and ritual action. As the middle ages progressed, the pattern of the church's worship became more rigidly defined, more closely identified with standard written texts and prescribed ritual actions. Add to this the contests and alliances between church and state, the realization that worship has political implications, and you have the mix out of which the English Reformation and the prayer book were born.

Arguably the most significant event of the post-resurrection church came in the legalization of Christianity by the emperor Constantine with the Edict of Milan in the year 313. Although it had grown significantly in the relative peace and stability of the late third century, under Constantine the church was suddenly transformed from a movement of small groups—sometimes seen as a Jewish sect and other times mistaken for one of the mystery religions or a subversive political element—to the officially sponsored religion of the emperor and his court.

Because of this transformation, within a very short time the church was receiving large numbers of converts. The shift can be seen dramatically in the changing architecture of Christian worship. In the pre-Constantinian period, Christians met in homes; the practices of their worship were shaped by this domestic, fairly intimate setting. Very quickly after Constantine's edict, however, the scene of Christian worship became the Roman basilica, a large public gathering place. The effect on the church's worship and thus on its self-understanding was profound.[1]

With the influx of numbers, the discipline of catechumenal formation began to break down. The sense of the church as another society began the wane, leading eventually to a virtual melding of church and state in medieval society. At the same time, the outward patterns of the church's liturgy—especially in regard to its leadership—began to acquire an overlay of ceremonial borrowed from late imperial culture. Congregations grew larger, as did the number of bishops and their assistant presbyters and deacons. The church was becoming a much more complicated institution and required different leadership and structures. No longer could it be automatically assumed, for instance, that a local bishop would be serving because of native gifts for presiding in the community; bishops were sometimes chosen for other, political or social reasons as well. Not every bishop had the gift for improvising the public prayer of the church, so the church began to move away from extemporaneous prayer (albeit according to definite models) toward the adoption of fixed texts.

～ Worship by the Book

It is at this point that the history of medieval liturgy begins, as the church entered a period of reshaping the liturgical patterns established in the early centuries. When Anglicans talk about liturgy, they generally do so with *The Book of Common Prayer* in mind—a set of uniform texts in one book outlining all our liturgical actions. Different congregations may use different kinds of ceremonial, but the texts are the same. Since the Reformation, the use of uniform texts has also been assumed by other liturgical churches, but such was not the case at the beginning of the early middle ages.

The period from the sixth to the eleventh centuries saw the rise of the power of the papacy and the gradual dominance of the church in Rome in western Europe. As Christianity spread throughout Europe, the liturgy came to be celebrated differently in different places. The patterns of baptism, eucharist, and daily prayer were essentially the same, but the way they were celebrated in, say, Gaul or Celtic Britain looked quite different from the way such rites were kept in Rome itself. In general, liturgy in the city of Rome was characterized by a simplicity and even a certain severity of style, both in ceremony and in its use of words. As the power of the papacy grew, the Roman form of the liturgy encountered liturgical patterns that had developed elsewhere, resulting in an elaboration of the Roman pattern that eventually became the norm throughout western Europe.

During the fourth and fifth centuries a succession of popes sponsored the writing and collection of prayer texts and liturgical directions in documents called sacramentaries and *ordines*, a process that continued through the next several centuries. One of the most significant compilers of these codifications in the sixth century was Pope Gregory the Great. He is particularly important for Anglicans because it was under his pontificate that Augustine of Canterbury was sent on his evangelizing mission to England. Among other things, Augustine brought Gregory's form of the Roman liturgy to England with him. Soon the Roman system of church governance met and overwhelmed the earlier Celtic shape of Christianity in Britain, and over time the Roman form of the liturgy became well-established in the monasteries and cathedrals of Britain.

This is not to suggest that in the early middle ages there was anything like absolute uniformity in the way the liturgy was celebrated—in Britain or anywhere else. We know, for example, that even in the city of Rome under Gregory the Great several versions of the liturgy were used. What we see in the early middle ages is the beginning of a process of codification that laid the groundwork for the development of the ideal of liturgical uniformity, an ideal that would later take hold in the Reformation and Counter-Reformation periods.

∾ The Work of the People
Becomes the Work of the Clergy

By the middle ages the Christianization of Europe had eliminated the serious preparation for baptism that the earlier catechumenate had embodied, and the popularity of the doctrine of original sin led to a more mechanical understanding of baptism as the cleansing of the effect of this sin. Baptism had ceased to make an obvious difference in the lives of newly baptized Christians, most of whom were infants of Christian parents; it was no longer experienced as a marking of one's entry into a distinct society. The church and the social order had largely become one entity. And as Richard Norris has remarked, if baptism ceases to differentiate, something else will.[2] That something else came to be entry into monastic life or ordination. The ordinary Christian began to resemble a consumer of services provided by a professional religious class, while the liturgy fell entirely into the hands of those trained specifically to do it. The sacraments became the "possession" of the clergy, just as the daily prayer of the church became the elaborated office of the monastic community.

The eleventh century in particular was a watershed in the history of the eucharist. A pronounced shift took place toward a more literal understanding of the transformation of the bread and wine into the body and blood of Christ, and theological speculation abounded on the nature of that transformation. At the same time, a more "transactional" understanding of the eucharist evolved, focusing not on the communal dimension of the meal or on making present the redemptive death and resurrection of Christ, but on offering a sacrifice for the sins of those present and the departed. This change coincided with a shift in popular piety emphasizing the suffering humanity of Christ, a shift that can be clearly seen in the art of the early middle ages: the earlier "imperial" depictions of Christ reigning in glory give way to the agonized depictions of medieval crucifixes.

During this period the laity became even further removed from the liturgical action: the eucharistic prayer was now said by the priest in an inaudible whisper (the language in any case was archaic Latin), the cup was withheld from the laity, and communions became infrequent in general because of a scrupulous concern about the bread and wine as sacred objects. It is once again in the architectural setting of the liturgy that the shift can be seen quite dramatically. From the original dining table of the earliest eucharistic meals to the freestanding altar tables of the Roman basilicas, the altar was now moved to the rear wall of churches. As the liturgy came to be seen more and more as the exclusive business of the priest, the position of the priest with his back to the people became universal. This distancing of the people from the eucharist became absolute in the system of private masses that eventually became a prominent feature of medieval church life—masses were required to be said daily by the clergy, whether any members of the congregation were present or not. This practice of saying a communal liturgy in private led to the curious discussion of whether the lone priest should also say the response "And with thy spirit" to the liturgical sentence "The Lord be with you."

The clergy conducted services from texts written, collected, and promulgated by their ecclesiastical authority, whether a particular bishop or the pope. Despite periodic efforts to enforce uniformity, regional differences persisted as services grew in number and ritual was elaborated. The monastic office in particular grew to unmanageable proportions; where it was also a requirement for secular clergy, it tended to be grouped into the two daily recitations of matins and vespers—perhaps an unwitting and dim reminder of the ancient pattern.[3]

The texts for all these rites had to be reproduced and maintained in manuscript form, and it is not difficult to imagine how local variations existed. In one form or another, by the time just prior to the Reformation, the principal books required to perform the liturgy of the church were these:

• The missal, containing the invariable text of the mass;

• The breviary, containing the daily office;

• The manual, containing the services used by priests, such as baptism, matrimony, and visitation of the sick;

• The pontifical, containing the services at which the bishop presided, such as confirmation and ordination; and

• The processional, containing music for processions on Sundays and other occasions.

In addition, the clergy needed books of ritual directions and the gospel and epistle readings, music for the liturgy, and books for governing conflicts in the calendar of feast days. For the laity—at least the wealthy and well-educated—there were devotional books to guide their prayers. These "primers" or "books of hours" contained prayers, devotions, psalms, and expositions of the meaning of the mass. By the fourteenth century these popular manuals existed in a multitude of forms to guide the private prayers of laity as they attended the liturgy. By the eve of the Reformation the laity had been effectively excluded from virtually any sense of active participation in the church's worship, and the early church's belief that they were the primary ministers of that worship was long forgotten.

∼ The Reformation

At its heart the Reformation was a liturgical movement. The reformers were as concerned about the state of the practical piety of ordinary worshipers as they were about biblical and sacramental theology.

They were troubled by the alienation of the laity from the worship of the church, and the most obvious changes resulting from the Protestant Reformation had to do with public worship. However, liturgical scholarship was not yet a discipline: the reformers, to varying degrees, tended to regard scripture as the record of the liturgical norms of the early church. Ironically, this view of the Bible led to the perpetuation of some of the very elements of medieval practice and piety that we now know were far removed from the ancient spirit of the liturgy as the work of *all* the holy people of God. In the Reformation the ancient patterns of Christian worship developed in new ways, some of which only served to further obscure those patterns. The ways in which the various reformers interpreted scripture profoundly affected the liturgy and worship of the church in their countries.

Martin Luther, the most significant reformer in Germany, was a conservative liturgist; as long as a feature of worship was not incompatible with scripture, it could be kept. He thus was not opposed to the retention of many features of the old rite—vestments, architecture, and ceremonial. Once medieval abuses had been corrected, the old practices could continue as long as they did not contradict scripture. Luther insisted that the liturgy be conducted in the vernacular, for he had a great concern for the practical education and participation of worshipers. To that end, he translated the mass into German and even provided music for its celebration.

In Geneva, on the other hand, John Calvin was more radical in his approach to worship. He believed that scripture gave a clear indication of how God wished to be worshiped. If a tradition was not specifically commanded by scripture, it was simply a human invention. But in ordering the life of his church in Geneva, even Calvin had to admit that scripture did not contain directions for every conceivable requirement of worship and so he had to accept the existence of *adiaphora*, things "added on." Preaching assumed a supreme importance in Calvin's church; like Luther, he too was passionate about the education of worshipers in what he considered a pure biblical faith.

Although the influence of continental reforms grew over time in England, the original roots of the English reformation were political rather than theological. Because of a confrontation with the pope, King Henry VIII had himself declared head of the church in England, seizing church property and threatening church convocations with dire consequences if the clergy did not support his programs. But in matters of public worship Henry allowed only cautious changes. Between 1532 to 1534—the time of Henry's decision to break with Rome—and Henry's death in 1546, scripture was allowed to be read in English, and some minor experimentation with services in English took place, including the use of the first English litany. Under Henry the medieval patterns of worship remained largely untouched. But the doors had been opened to the work of the continental reformers, and they began to have a deep impact on men like Henry's Archbishop of Canterbury, Thomas Cranmer. The stage was set for deeper liturgical reforms.

∾ The Prayer Book is Born

In 1547, as a boy of eleven, Edward VI came to the throne. His advisers were reform-minded men and began almost immediately the process of revising the liturgy. The first step was to experiment with the entire service in English, but this was simply a prelude to structural changes. The cup was restored to the laity in an English supplement to the Latin missal, "The Order of Communion." A catechism appeared. Cranmer produced a revision of the breviary, reducing the complex monastic office to a daily pattern of morning and evening prayer. All these changes paved the way for the first *Book of Common Prayer*.

In 1548 a committee of "learned men" was charged with producing a "godly order" of worship for use in England. It is likely that Thomas Cranmer was the principal drafter of this new order, incorporating into it elements from ancient sources, the rites of the eastern church, and the work of contemporary reformers. And in January of 1549 Parliament passed the Act of Uniformity, making the first prayer book the official order of worship in England. It had the impressively lengthy title of *The Book of the Common Prayer and Administration of the Sacraments and other Rites and Ceremonies of the Church, after the Use of the Church of England*. It was intended to replace the missal, the breviary, the manual, and the processional, and represented a major simplification of medieval practice.

The prayer book of 1549 was in many respects a conservative reform of liturgical patterns. The structural shape of the eucharist, baptism, and the daily office was recognizable as that of the old Latin rite, but greatly simplified. Although there were significant innovations—such as the reading of large portions of the Bible at Morning and Evening Prayer—the tone of the services largely remained that of the late medieval church. What was radically new was the fact that these rites were now considered to be *common* prayer. What had formerly been available only to the clergy was now printed and put into the hands of every worshiper. And in this change was the beginning of a genuine rediscovery of the most basic Christian liturgical principle, namely that the worship of the church is the public business of the whole church, not the private domain of the clergy. While the domination of the liturgy by the clergy certainly continued in England, the first *Book of Common Prayer* was a significant step toward a recovery of the ancient pattern.

No one was satisfied with the 1549 prayer book. (All prayer books seem to suffer this fate!) It fell victim to the politics and religious upheavals of its time, as some felt this prayer book was only a first step toward further changes while others wanted to return to the old rite. It was during the Reformation that public prayer came to be not only a sign of religious orthodoxy—whether Protestant or Catholic—but also of allegiance to the state.

In 1552 the second prayer book of Edward VI was authorized and required to be used. It moved decidedly in the direction of Calvinist practice, and many of the ceremonies authorized by the 1549 book were now abolished. Any suggestion that the eucharist was an offering was eliminated. The implication in the 1552 prayer book is that the presence of Christ is to be found in the heart of the worshiper, rather than in the eucharistic bread and wine. A simple said service was the norm. The book was in use only eight months, for in 1553 Edward VI died and the staunch Roman Catholic Mary Tudor ascended the throne, immediately restoring the Latin rite.

After three bloody years, the reign of Mary ended as Elizabeth I came to the throne, and with her returned the prayer book. The revised prayer book of 1559 was an attempt to make and keep the peace. Elizabeth inherited a volatile situation in which political and religious issues were hard to untangle. Proceeding with caution and great political sophistication, she was able to achieve a remarkable solution. The 1559 prayer book restored some of the provisions of the 1549 book (including the use of vestments such as the alb, chasuble, and cope) and eliminated an inflammatory clause from the litany against the bishop of Rome. Doctrinally, Elizabeth's book took a carefully considered road between extremes. In 1549 the words of administration of Holy Communion had been "The Body of our Lord Jesus Christ which was given for thee, preserve thy body and soul unto everlasting life." In 1552 the words were changed to "Take and eat this in remembrance that Christ died for thee, and feed on him in thy heart, by faith with thanksgiving." In the 1559 book, the two phrases were combined and have been included in every subsequent revision. The compromise is a classic example of the pragmatic spirit of Anglicanism in practice.

This pragmatic approach to Christianity is deeply rooted in the genius of Elizabeth's settlement. She is often quoted as having insisted that in her realm "windows would not be made into men's souls." Elizabeth wanted the church to be a sign and agent of unity in England, rather than a cause for sedition and bloodshed. The divisive and even violent results of Reformation doctrinal controversies were all too obvious, both in England and in Europe. Worship according to a single prayer book was to be the distinguishing feature of church life in England. Rather than inquisitions into the privately held theological convictions of her people, she would insist only on the public practice of worship according to *The Book of Common Prayer.* The prayer book was rooted deep in the liturgical tradition of the pre-Reformation church, but was obviously responsive to the new political realities of post-Reformation England.

The Book of Common Prayer was revised again in 1604 when James I succeeded Elizabeth and yet again in 1662 when the monarchy was restored with Charles II after the commonwealth period: it is this 1662 prayer book that is still the authorized book of the Church of England. It is a testament to the durability of the Elizabethan settlement that these subsequent revisions involved only modest changes to the book of 1559. Anyone familiar with the 1979 *Book of Common Prayer* will recognize at least the roots it shares with Elizabeth's book.

What emerged in sixteenth-century Anglicanism was a version of the ancient pattern of Christian worship. As expressed in the prayer book, this pattern was characterized by simplicity and the ideal of common prayer, a rhythm of daily praying with psalms and scripture, and eucharistic worship on the Lord's Day. The prayer book pattern would be challenged by Puritans and Roman Catholics, and disregarded and misunderstood by Anglicans themselves. But for many Christians it represents an authentic restatement of the heart of Christian practice.

∼ The Prayer Book Tradition

To be an Anglican is to be shaped by a tradition of worship, one that takes seriously not only gifts from the past, but the experience of contemporary people and the challenges they face. We have a tradition of worship that is deeply sacramental, and affirms that God has entered history and continues to act within human lives. We shape our life together as a church out of our faith that God has made this world the place where salvation happens. Again, this characteristic of Anglicanism was given its definitive shape at the end of the sixteenth century out of the rough and tumble of Reformation controversies. In his work *Laws of Ecclesiastical Polity*, the theologian Richard Hooker mapped out a path for Anglicanism between the extremes of papal and Puritan claims—a path between the wholesale return to the encrusted tradition of Rome or the sweeping aside of centuries of Christian tradition. This path, often called the *via media* or middle way, seeks to honor the church's tradition while engaging newly emerging realities of the present. Hooker believed that the Incarnation of Christ was an ongoing reality and that Christians participate in it through the sacramental life of the church. In this way, he was reframing the earliest patterns of Christian experience expressed in worship.

Anglicanism is as much a spiritual stance as anything else. It is a way of engaging the world from the vantage point of the Incarnation—the faith that God has become enfleshed and come among us in Jesus

Christ, the faith that the church is in some sense the ongoing self-expression of the body of Christ. This rootedness in the doctrine of the Incarnation gives Anglicanism the possibility of extraordinary courage when facing a world of change and challenge. Insofar as it embodies this incarnational faith, *The Book of Common Prayer* in all its various revisions stands as a sign of a tradition that is very much alive.

Chapter 4

The American Prayer Book

> "The people of this congregation (I mean ye Church's real Friends, ye communicants) universally disapprove of ye new Book...."
> —*Thomas Clagget, first Bishop of Maryland, reporting on the reception of the Proposed Prayer Book of 1786.*[1]

In a parish where a friend of mine was serving as rector, the worship committee had begun some liturgical innovation involving inclusive language rites and a new position for the altar. There was a lot of consternation in the congregation about the changes. One day my friend reported to me a conversation he had had with a long-time member of the parish who supported the changes. After a particularly intense parish meeting he said wearily to his parishioner, "Why are liturgical changes always so hard?" The parishioner looked at her rector and replied, "Why shouldn't they be hard? People know that when you change the way they worship, they might have to change other things too...like their lives." Liturgical revision, like any change that matters, is almost never popular—with clergy or laity.

I once asked the administrator of the parish in which I served, a woman who had grown up in the Episcopal Church, how she would describe the difference between the 1928 and the 1979 prayer books. She said that when she was growing up with the 1928 book, God was always "up there" somewhere, and we were poor sinners who had to be very careful because we might say the wrong thing. However, after using the current prayer book for a number of years she had a much greater sense that God is here among us.

I think she captured the fundamental difference between the two prayer books well. In its language and its theology the 1928 prayer book reflects a sixteenth-century western society that was largely Christian—at least in name and culture—and an essentially medieval understanding of the nature of sin and redemption. The 1979 book represents a deep shift in the direction of a more ancient, biblical view of God and God's relationship in Christ to the church and the world. To understand this shift and the prayer book we have today we need to look at the history that produced it, beginning with the dramatic changes of the colonial church's break with the Church of England in the eighteenth century.

~ An Independent Church

The American Revolution brought a host of challenges for Anglicans in the former colonies. Not the least of these was the need to revise *The Book of Common Prayer.* Some issues were immediately obvious:

prayers for the monarch and the oath of loyalty to the crown required at ordination, for example, were clearly politically inappropriate for an American church. But there were other issues of theology and practice that would play a large role in the American revision. Over the next two hundred years the prayer book pattern was to be reshaped in significant ways by an Anglican church facing pastoral and missionary challenges in a rapidly changing new world.

The English 1662 prayer book was in use throughout the colonies before the Revolution; the colonial church was, after all, the Church of England. After the events of 1776 some assumed that only a modest revision of the established English prayer book was required. But other, reforming influences were at work among church people during this period. Of particular importance was the prayer book tradition of the non-juror, Scottish church: non-jurors were those who would not give their allegiance to the new monarchs William and Mary after James II was forced to leave the throne. They formed an outlawed Anglican church that, like the American church, was free from the oath of uniformity to the established English prayer book.

This Scottish strand began to influence the American situation early on, particularly in New England. It did so most obviously with the consecration of Samuel Seabury of Connecticut as the first bishop of the Episcopal Church in the United States. As a result of the English bishops' initial refusal to ordain bishops for the American church, Seabury was ordained to the episcopate in 1784 by bishops of the non-juring Episcopal Church in Scotland. He promised in return to try to persuade the church in the United States to adopt the Scottish rite for the celebration of the eucharist.

⌇ *Scottish Influence*

The liturgy of the Episcopal Church in Scotland has a rather different history from that of the English prayer book. Henry VIII was never king and Elizabeth I was never queen of Scotland. The Scottish reformation under John Knox followed its own course. When James VI of Scotland succeeded Elizabeth as James I of England, he attempted to bring the Scottish church into conformity with England by having Scottish bishops consecrated and by introducing the prayer book. In spite of the attempts of James and his son Charles I, the English prayer book of 1604 was never accepted in Scotland, and the Scottish bishops, with the approval of the Archbishop of Canterbury under Charles I, William Laud, produced the Scottish prayer book of 1637, a book more in the spirit of 1549 and Laud's own views.

The Scottish prayer book of 1637 contained a number of changes to the English prayer books that are still familiar to worshipers using Rite I in the 1979 book today. The collection, along with the bread and wine, is to be offered "upon the Lord's Table." The prayer over the bread and wine is called the Prayer of Consecration and includes an invocation of the Holy Spirit upon the gifts, known as the *epiclesis*: "of thy almighty goodness, vouchsafe to bless and sanctify, with thy Word and Holy Spirit, these thy gifts and creatures of bread and wine." In this prayer book the words of institution are followed not immediately by communion (as in the English books since 1552), but by the Memorial or Prayer of Oblation: "Here we offer and present unto thee, O Lord, our selves, our souls and bodies. . . . " The Lord's Prayer is introduced by the familiar words "As our Lord Jesus Christ hath taught us, we are bold to say," and the Lord's Prayer is followed by the Prayer of Humble Access; in the English prayer books this prayer comes immediately after the *Sanctus* and before the rest of the eucharistic prayer.

Although it was to have long-lasting influence, the 1637 Scottish book was short-lived in Scotland. In the supercharged religious and political climate of the time its introduction caused riots, and it was abandoned almost as soon as it was introduced. Its influence, however, was to be significant on both the 1662 prayer book of the Church of England and especially on the 1764 revision of the Scottish prayer book, the version used at the consecration of Samuel Seabury.

The 1764 Scottish revision incorporates material and insights from a variety of ancient sources. In the early 1700s Anglican liturgical scholars had begun to look seriously at what was then known about the liturgical patterns of the early church. Some scholars began to promote a recovery of what they understood some of those practices to be. Because of its non-juror status, the church in Scotland was freer to experiment with and adopt these usages than the church in England, and versions of the liturgy were produced in the form of "wee bookies." For the first time a deliberate attempt was made by an organized body of Anglicans to create liturgy according to ancient patterns, prefiguring the project at the heart of the liturgical reforms of our own time.[2]

Perhaps the most significant contribution of the Scottish prayer book revision of 1764 was the attempt to recover the ancient sacrificial pattern of the eucharist: the offering of bread and wine in thanksgiving for all that God has done for us in Christ, together with the invocation of the Holy Spirit to make them a present reality.[3] This Scottish rite placed the words of offering and invocation in the eucharist where they still appear in Rite I of the 1979 *Book of Common Prayer:*

> We, thy humble servants, do celebrate and make here before thy divine Majesty, with these thy holy gifts, which we now offer unto thee, the memorial thy Son hath commanded us to make....
>
> ...vouchsafe to bless and sanctify, with thy Word and Holy Spirit, these thy gifts and creatures of bread and wine.... (BCP 335)

⌒ The First American Prayer Book

For their part, Anglicans in the newly independent United States found themselves in a unique situation. The question for them was how to remain Anglicans faithful to the *tradition* of *The Book of Common Prayer* while still revising that tradition in light of their new social and political context. They were suddenly (and disconcertingly) free to do just that, without reference to Parliament or the crown. Members of the church in the United States found the prayer book in their own hands, suddenly called upon to make decisions about it. The church was free to revise the official prayer book, taking into consideration those theological understandings that made the greatest sense in the new world. Liturgical scholarship and the freedom to revise would be the driving factors in a future of ongoing prayer book revisions.

In 1785 a convention of Anglicans from the states south of New England met in Philadelphia. Samuel Seabury in Connecticut refused to attend in part because proposals for organizing the newly independent church did not provide adequately for the place of bishops in church governance, but none of the New England states was represented at this first post-Revolution convention. Nevertheless, this first attempt at organizing the life of the fledgling Episcopal Church recognized the necessity of taking steps to revise the prayer book. It authorized William White, later to be bishop of Pennsylvania, with the assistance of William Smith of Maryland and others, to work on a revision. This they did, and later that same year produced what was to be adopted by the southern states as the proposed prayer book of 1786.

This book was essentially a revision of the 1662 prayer book—in the direction of the Latitudinarianism of the eighteenth century. Influenced by the rationalism and deism of the time, the prayer book of 1786 deemphasized distinctive doctrines such as the Trinity and the atonement and offered a less exalted view of the sacraments and episcopacy. The most obvious changes from the 1662 book—apart from removing prayers for the monarch—were the omission of the Nicene and Athanasian creeds and the removal of the phrase "He descended into hell" from the Apostles' Creed. Other than these changes, the proposed book of

1786 contained only a few other minor rearrangements of material from the English prayer book.

As with virtually every revision before and after it, the proposed book of 1786 was not popular. It was objected to by some on the grounds that it had been prepared by a convention without the authority of a bishop, by others that it changed the creeds, and by others still that it was simply not the book they had always used! The suspicion that this proposed book was in fact the final, unalterable book for the newly independent church also worked to undermine its reception.[4] The English bishops, to whom the southern states looked for episcopal consecration, objected to the elimination of the Nicene and Athanasian creeds and to the alteration of the Apostles' Creed. It is difficult to imagine how any revision could have been received with enthusiasm, given the political and ecclesiastical realities of the time—Tories and patriots, Latitudinarians and advocates of traditional liturgical forms, all trying to form one unified church. The English solution of public adherence to one common liturgy was thrown into serious question in the political situation of the new nation, and yet the Anglican pattern of Christianity demanded common prayer. The unity, even the continuing existence, of the church in the United States demanded a new prayer book.

The first General Convention of the Protestant Episcopal Church met in Philadelphia on September 29, 1789. It was able to meet at all in large measure because the southern states gave up their commitment to the proposed book of 1786 with its elements Seabury and others in New England found objectionable. By all accounts it was as diverse a gathering as any General Convention has been to the present day. There were delegates who thought the 1662 prayer book only needed slight revision to suit the new country's situation. There were Latitudinarians who wanted references to the Trinity eliminated and all prayer addressed simply to the Father. There were those who advocated revision according to the Scottish pattern, incorporating elements from ancient liturgies and Eastern Orthodoxy. In the end, remarkably, it took the convention just ten days to produce a revision of the prayer book for the church in the United States of America.

There were disputes about the inclusion of the Athanasian Creed, about the "descent into hell" clause in the Apostles' Creed, and about the way the Psalter would be presented for use. But the most significant issue, in terms of its importance for the emergence of a distinctively American prayer book pattern, was the adoption of the Scottish model of the Prayer of Consecration in the celebration of Holy Communion. The eucharistic prayer that finally appeared in the first American prayer book relies on elements from the communion rite introduced by Bishop Seabury in Connecticut and on revisions that had come into use in Maryland and Pennsylvania.[5] This prayer represents an important recovery of the ancient Christian pattern of giving thanks over bread and wine; its incorporation was the result of liturgical scholarship and the newly independent church's ability and willingness to revise its public worship without legal constraints. In fact, the most important legacy of the first American prayer book may be simply the fact of its existence. The church saw that it was possible to revise Anglican liturgy without reference to governmental authority. As Anglicanism has grown from its established church roots into a worldwide communion of independent and interdependent churches, it has explored this freedom with more and more confidence. The prayer book has flourished in a church that is free to revise it.

The book adopted at the General Convention of 1789 and published in 1790 bore the title that has appeared on every subsequent revision: *The Book of Common Prayer, and Administration of the Sacraments, and Other Rites and Ceremonies of the Church, According to the Use of the Protestant Episcopal Church in the United States of America: together with the Psalter, or Psalms of David.* In the 1979 *Book of Common Prayer* the title is somewhat shortened to read *According to the use of the Episcopal Church.*

The American prayer book of 1789 would be in use for the next hundred years. While the various offices and rites are arranged in the 1789 book in a different order than in the current book, its pattern of worship would be recognizable to anyone familiar with the 1979 prayer book: a calendar and lectionary for the liturgical year, the orders for daily Morning and Evening Prayer, The Lord's Supper or Holy Communion, Baptism and Confirmation, Holy Matrimony, Visitation of the Sick, and Burial, a catechism, and a collection of prayers for various occasions.

However, although the pattern and text of the rites might be familiar to a contemporary user of the prayer book, the style in which those rites were celebrated—their architectural setting and ceremonial—probably would not. In churches of the colonial period, a typical arrangement would be for Morning Prayer to be read from a triple-decker pulpit on the north wall of a building in the Georgian or "meeting-house" colonial style. On Sundays, Morning Prayer would be followed by the Litany and Holy Communion, although in popular practice it was usually Ante-Communion: the service of Holy Communion only through the readings and sermon. Music would consist of metrical psalms and simple hymns accompanied possibly by a group of instrumentalists. It is to this rather bare and yet lengthy and invariable pattern that the movement can be traced in the next century demanding greater flexibility and enrichment of prayer book worship—in other words, further revision of the prayer book.

~ Nineteenth-Century Revisions

Several years ago I watched a now rather outdated video with my youth group called *Mass Appeal*. I later told a friend about how much I had enjoyed the film (although the members of the youth group howled with laughter at the clothes and haircuts), when my friend stopped me and said, "You know, isn't it funny how they had to film this story about Roman Catholic priests in the setting of an Episcopal Church? Did you know that the church in the movie is an Episcopal Church? After all, they had to use a church that looked like a church."

The images many people have about what worship in an Episcopal church looks like—vested choirs and processions, candles flickering at altars set in long divided chancels, organ music, pseudo-Gothic architecture, and the Holy Eucharist as the principal serv-ice—can be traced to reforms in the nineteenth centu-ry that took the prayer book tradition and reshaped it. Some of these movements had to do with social changes, some with changing artistic tastes and fash-ions, some with scholarly inquiry in theology and liturgy, and some with shifts in piety, but all made their mark and contributed to the next stage in prayer book revision: the prayer book of 1892 and on to the 1928 prayer book.

One key factor in the story of any prayer book revision is the people who lead the call for change, and this is no less true of the revisions in the nineteenth century. The early story of *The Book of Common Prayer* is dominated by kings, queens, and archbishops, by actions of Parliament and royal councils. I can imag-ine the beleaguered residents of some English village waiting for the next edict as to how they were going to worship *this* year. Likewise, the figures who loom large in the story of the first hundred years or so of the American prayer book are clergymen. While ordi-nary churchgoers were certainly interested in and affected by changes in the prayer book, leadership for the changes came largely from the clergy. It is true to say that the clergy called for changes in the prayer book in response to what they saw as pastoral needs, but the role of laypersons was to react or adapt to the changes initiated by their leaders. To tell the story of nineteenth-century prayer book revision is largely to name prominent clergymen and scholars. As we shall see, it is not until the revisions of the twentieth cen-tury that a very different pattern emerges, with the contributions of laypersons calling for reform equaling those of the clergy.

By the middle of the nineteenth century it was obvious that the 1789 prayer book was not meeting the needs of a church trying to minister to a fast-changing population. That century witnessed the Civil War, an influx of large numbers of immigrants, and a rapidly industrializing economy, while the challenge of biblical criticism and evolutionary theory began to be felt in the church. The Catholic Revival, with its origins in the English Oxford Movement, was leading to a deeper appreciation of the sacraments and a renewed interest in medieval liturgy and the study of liturgy in general.[6] Ritualism, a child of the Catholic Revival, was eventually to transform thoroughly the physical fabric, ceremonial, and music of the Episcopal Church. It is startling to realize what an innovation it was in the middle of the nineteenth century to place a cross on the Holy Table of an Episcopal Church. In England, ritualism was to cause sometimes violent controversies about what enrichments were and were not *legally* permissible. Although there were certainly controversies in the United States over the introduction of vestments, crosses, and so forth, the fact that the rubrics and canons of the American church leave such matters largely to taste and custom helped the practices of ritualism to spread quite broadly.

The need for greater flexibility in worship was perhaps most apparent in urban centers and on the missionary frontiers. In these settings, the sheer weight of lengthy Sunday services was impractical for populations with neither the time nor the inclination to attend them as traditionally presented. The clergy began to ask for greater freedom to use the prayer book in more flexible ways. In 1853 William Augustus Muhlenberg gave formal voice to these requests by calling on the General Convention to authorize flexibility in the use of prayer book services and a greater sensitivity to the ecumenical opportunities for the Episcopal Church in a multidenominational, multicultural society. In his own work as head of an influential boys' school and later as the founder of the Church of the Holy Communion in New York City, he advocated enriching worship with music, flowers, and the colors of the liturgical year. It was Muhlenberg who introduced the practice of singing parts of the service, chanting psalms, and placing the altar in a central position, with the pulpit to one side. At his church he separated the celebration of Holy Communion from Morning Prayer and the Litany and began to celebrate the eucharist weekly.

Muhlenberg's interest in the beauty of worship was tied to a deep concern for the poor and the needs of urban working people. This responsiveness to changing needs and circumstances marked a new perspective in the Episcopal Church on the deep links between liturgy and the lives of church members. In a form called a "memorial" Muhlenberg requested permission from the General Convention for greater flexibility in using the prayer book. Although the request was not granted, it was to exercise great influence in paving the way for future liturgical reform. One specific outcome of the memorial was that three years later the House of Bishops explicitly noted that Morning Prayer, the Litany, and Holy Communion were distinct services that could be conducted separately. Until the 1979 prayer book, the typical Sunday morning schedule of worship in many Episcopal parishes was an early celebration of the eucharist followed by a main service of Morning Prayer. This pattern can be traced to the bishops' provision—an unintended warping of the traditional Christian pattern of *daily* morning and evening prayer, and a principal eucharist on the Lord's Day.

Calls for liturgical flexibility and enrichment were made at successive General Conventions through the last half of the nineteenth century, but it was not until forty years after Muhlenberg's memorial that the prayer book was finally revised. A key figure in this next stage of revision was William Reed Huntington, the rector of Grace Church in New York City and a leader in the House of Deputies of the General Convention. His persistent calls for revision began the process in 1880 that led in 1883 to the issuing of a prayer book for trial use, known as *The Book Annexed*. During the three-year trial period that followed there were many suggestions for liturgical changes that went far beyond simply shortening services, including eliminating the Ten Commandments at the beginning of Holy Communion, reciting the Nicene Creed in the first-person plural, and placing the sermon after the gospel rather than after the creed (where it had appeared in every prayer book since 1549).[7]

The mood of the General Conventions of 1883 and 1886 turned cautious, however. There was growing criticism of many of the proposals, and tension around controversies stemming from both the Catholic Revival and liberalism probably made this conservative mood inevitable. Finally, the General

Convention in 1892 approved a modest revision of the prayer book—a revision so modest that the most noticeable change from the 1789 book is that the *Magnificat* and the *Nunc Dimittis*, traditional canticles at Evening Prayer, appear for the first time in the American prayer book. Though the changes were few, the 1892 book did make it clear that liturgical revision was both necessary and possible: some kind of change in the church's worship was inevitable in response to the circumstances of modern life. Worship had to take into account the realities of large-scale immigration, missionary work among black and Native American populations, evangelism on the frontier, and the growth of city slums.

～ 1928 and Beyond

The prayer book of 1892 was in use just twenty-one years before the process of revision formally began again. At the General Convention of 1913 memorials were presented by the dioceses of California and Arizona to appoint a joint commission to begin the process of "revising and enriching" the prayer book. There were predictable reactions to this call for revision, ranging from enthusiasm through caution to stalwart opposition. Again, the pace of change and world events were cited as more pressing concerns. But the advocates of revision were not concerned with liturgical niceties divorced from the real issues faced by ordinary worshipers. They were convinced that those very issues demanded new ways of praying. And people knew then, as we know now, that if they changed the way they worshiped, they might have to change their lives too.

The proposed revisions were significantly more substantial than previous changes in the prayer book, and they were hammered out at successive General Conventions between 1913 and 1928. The most influential leader in the revision process this time was Edward Lambe Parsons, later bishop of California and professor of theology and liturgy at Church Divinity School of the Pacific. He is responsible for writing new prayers for the 1928 book for social justice, for the "family of nations," and the collect for Independence Day. The 1928 prayer book also reflected other concerns of the day and the changing attitudes of society: there is a much greater concern overall for social justice, the marriage service drops the word "obey" from the wife's vows, and the derogatory reference to "the Jews" is dropped from the third collect for Good Friday. At the same time, provision is made in the Visitation of the Sick for laying on hands and anointing, and there is a greater sensitivity to ecumenical concerns.

Some charged that changes in the 1928 book went too far in the direction of Roman Catholicism. This is because propers were added for the celebration of the eucharist at burials and marriages, for example, as well as prayers for the dead, and the Lord's Prayer became the conclusion of the Prayer of Consecration in Holy Communion. But these changes were made as a result of contemporary scholarship rather than from the influence of Anglo-Catholics looking to Roman Catholic practice. Anglo-Catholics wanted to include elements such as the *Agnus Dei* and *Benedictus qui venit* (the "Blessed is he who comes in the name of the Lord" at the conclusion of the *Sanctus*), as well as a rubric permitting the reservation of the sacrament, but these additions were rejected.[8]

In what may seem like a curious footnote to us today, some of the most widespread objections to the 1928 book focused on the preface to the Lord's Prayer at the conclusion of the Prayer of Consecration. The 1925 General Convention had agreed on the words "And now as our Savior Christ hath taught us, let us say. . . . " The joint commission changed that phrase to the now familiar, "And now, as our Savior Christ hath taught us, we are bold to say. . . . " This is the wording in Samuel Seabury's version of the Scottish liturgy and in the 1549 prayer book. The effect is to make the Lord's Prayer the conclusion of the eucharistic prayer, still addressed to the Father, according to an ancient pattern. But the change was seized on by some as evidence that this book was leading down the path to Rome.[9]

⁀ The Liturgical Movement

At the same time that Episcopalians were working on the revision of the prayer book, an ecumenical movement began that would transform the worship and self-understanding of all the Christian churches in the twentieth century. Over the last fifty years in particular, the Liturgical Movement has grown into what one writer calls the "Liturgical Revolution."[10] Its roots can be traced all the way back to the Reformation and resulting scholarship—either in attempts to bolster positions on one side or the other, or to return to some imagined pristine biblical or early church practice.

For a variety of reasons, the Reformation period saw renewed interest in the historical development of

Christian worship. In order to support one or another position or church practice, early church source materials began to be collected, providing a growing body of evidence regarding worship in the first centuries of the church's life. By the nineteenth century it had become obvious to some scholars that the liturgical life of the church was very far removed from what it had originally been, both in spirit and in practical detail. The essential shape of the pattern of Christian worship had been almost totally obscured in both Protestant and Roman Catholic churches.

It is hard to overstate the impact that the recovery of descriptions of worship and texts from the early church has had on the way we worship today. Copies of these important texts had been gathering dust in monastic libraries for centuries. In an age when we have instant access to historical materials from every time and culture, we are amazed to know that Mozart wrote all his works without ever having heard Bach's *Brandenburg* Concerti—they were lying unknown in a library. Likewise, it is hard to imagine that Archbishop Thomas Cranmer, the author of the first prayer book, did not know many of the texts that today are considered fundamental to an understanding of the principles of Christian worship. The recovery of those texts caused a revolution in our celebration of liturgy on a scale equal to Cranmer's pioneering work in his own day.

The first stirrings of the modern Liturgical Movement occurred in Roman Catholic monastic communities during the first years of this century. Names associated with the earliest stages of the movement include the Benedictine monks of Solesmes in France and their abbot, Prosper Guèranger, and Dom Lambert Beauduin in Belgium. In Germany and Austria the movement is associated with the abbeys of Maria Laach and Klosterneuberg, with individuals such as Ildefons Herwegen, Odo Casel, and Pius Parsch. There were subtle and important differences between them, but what they had in common was a passion for recovering a sense of the fundamental pattern at the heart of Christian worship, a pattern they discerned clearly in the witness of the early church but not in the liturgy of their own time.

At first, the Liturgical Movement had little direct impact on worship in the Anglican Communion. But beginning in the 1930s in England, pioneers such as Henry de Candole and A. G. Hebert began to publish works applying the insights of the continental movement to the Church of England. Their work was to promote the development of what came to be called "the parish communion," a genuinely participative "family eucharist" that was the principal Sunday service. The movement in England embraced more than just liturgical questions, however. It focused on the connections between worship and social action, the implications of the liturgy for the life of Christians in the world. "Liturgy means the activity of the people of God," wrote Henry de Candole, "which is primarily a corporate common activity of the whole fellowship."[11] That corporate action was seen increasingly to stand in fairly stark contrast to the growing individualism of the modern world, a situation that the rigid and clericalized worship of the Anglican Church was incapable of adequately addressing.

In the United States, the name of William Palmer Ladd is most closely associated with the spread of the Liturgical Movement and its impact on worship in the Episcopal Church. Ladd taught at Berkeley Divinity School in New Haven, Connecticut, from 1904 to 1941, where he actively promoted the works of those in the European Liturgical Movement. He was especially concerned about the social implications of the liturgy. In 1942 an important collection of Ladd's essays were published titled *Prayer Book Interleaves*. The thrust of these essays was to argue for a revolution in liturgical spirituality by recapturing the profoundly corporate pattern of the early church's worship—a project begun but hardly realized in the Reformation. And this corporate pattern was essential to the church's mission, argued Ladd, since the church was increasingly irrelevant to the lives of men and women. How could it not be, with infrequent celebrations of the eucharist in antique language dominated by the clergy? How could it be otherwise, with baptisms routinely conducted as private family affairs or events only for the Sunday school?

Ladd's influence was significant, but he was not alone. Ladd's friend and student, Massey Shepherd, was to be one of the driving forces behind the 1979 prayer book. Charles Winfred Douglas had an enormous impact on the worship of the Episcopal Church as well. Through his influence in the production of *The Hymnal 1940*, with its repertoire of liturgical music designed to be sung by congregations, he brought to bear on popular practice the heart of the Liturgical Movement: the vision of the liturgy as the shared work of priest and people. The publication in 1937 of

The American Prayer Book by Edward Lambe Parsons and Bayard Hale Jones, who both served on the Standing Liturgical Commission, brought the insights of the liturgical scholarship of the time to the attention of a whole generation of future church leaders.

In the Episcopal Church the Liturgical Movement found its greatest and most persistent advocate in an organization known as Associated Parishes for Liturgy and Mission. Begun in 1946 by a group of clergy who wanted to find practical ways to implement the principles of the Liturgical Movement, given the realities of parish life and the 1928 prayer book, it was to exercise enormous influence over the next thirty years leading to the 1979 *Book of Common Prayer*.[12] Through its publications and conferences Associated Parishes was an early advocate of many liturgical practices that have become commonplace: the parish eucharist as the principal Sunday service, offertory and gospel processions, freestanding altars, the recovery of ancient patterns of worship for Holy Week. Associated Parishes has counted among its members many of the key participants in modern prayer book revision, including those who produced the 1979 book.

∾ Ongoing Revision and the 1979 Prayer Book

The influential nineteenth-century Anglican theologian Frederick Denison Maurice once said, "I hope you will never hear from me any such phrase as our 'excellent or incomparable Liturgy.' . . . I do not think we are to praise the Liturgy, but to use it."[13] Over the course of one hundred fifty years, the Episcopal Church had moved from understanding its pattern of Christian worship as a monolithic, invariable, and unchanging set of texts and ritual actions, to a sense that flexibility, variety, and change were not only inevitable but desirable if the church was to accomplish its mission. By the second half of the twentieth century *The Book of Common Prayer* was increasingly seen as a distinctive and living pattern of Christian life and worship that could change, rather than as a sacred object in and of itself.

From 1928 to 1979 there was an explosion of theological, biblical, and liturgical scholarship, as well as social and political upheavals in the world and in the church. With the adoption of the 1928 prayer book came the realization that liturgical change was to be a constant need in the church's life: in order to use the prayer book effectively, the church must reshape it time and again. The General Convention of 1928 created the Standing Liturgical Commission, whose responsibility it would be to continue the study of liturgical matters and to recommend future revisions to meet the church's ongoing needs. The 1979 *Book of Common Prayer* is the result of their work, and reflects a church coming to terms with the modern world by exploring its patterns of worship at deeper historical and theological levels.

I came into the Episcopal Church as a teenager in the 1970s, the period of "The Green Book" and "The Zebra Book"—trial usage prayer books (named for their covers) that led the way to the official adoption of the 1979 prayer book. The parish in Sturgis, Michigan, that welcomed me into the Episcopal Church had a long history of Anglo-Catholic worship. In fact, for many years it had used *The Anglican Missal* for Sunday and weekday celebrations of the eucharist.[14] The main service on Sundays was solemn mass, with incense, three sacred ministers dressed in medieval vestments, and squadrons of acolytes. The entire liturgy was sung, the gospel was chanted from a lavishly decorated book, and bells were rung at both the *Sanctus* and the words of institution in the eucharistic prayer. The building itself made the tradition of the parish's worship unmistakable: a large crucifix over the altar with its tabernacle for the reservation of the sacrament, statues of Joseph and Mary with Jesus, the stations of the cross on the walls. I did not realize until later in my life that it was surprising to find an Episcopal parish with this kind of tradition quite happily using "The Green Book." Looking back, however, it makes sense.

The Anglo-Catholic tradition was just one variation among several that had taken root and grown in Anglican worship. Throughout its life the basic prayer book pattern has been enriched, interpreted, and enacted in a wide variety of ways. Rubrics have been ignored or bent, additions have been made, and some provisions ignored—all of this in Anglo-Catholic, broad church, or evangelical fashion, without following "the letter of the law" of the official *Book of Common Prayer.* For instance, it would have been virtually impossible to find any parish, of whatever tradition, following the order prescribed in the 1928 (and earlier) prayer books of singing the *Gloria* at the *end* of Holy Communion.

What came to pass in the revision process leading to the 1979 prayer book was, among many other things, an honest admission of this variety and a recognition that it was not necessarily inconsistent with the deeply embedded pattern of worship at the heart of the prayer book tradition. "The Green Book" and other trial liturgies allowed for and gave official encouragement to the kind of variety that my parish had unofficially practiced for years. What these books also began to foster was not taste in ceremonial, music, or piety, but a greater clarity about the deep structures of the prayer book tradition and their implications for Christian life and witness today.

By the early 1960s it had become obvious to many people that the church had to revise *The Book of Common Prayer.* What was less obvious was the precise shape that revision would take. Both the church and the world were undergoing profound changes, and perspective is hard to achieve in the midst of a revolution. The forces of the Liturgical Movement, ecumenism, and biblical scholarship all combined to provide powerful new models of what was possible in Christian worship. The Second Vatican Council in 1963 had called for sweeping changes in Roman Catholic practice, but other branches of the Anglican Communion had also undertaken significant revisions of their prayer books, as had other liturgical churches. These changes reflected the broad outlines of the Liturgical Movement: an insistence on baptism as the fundamental sacrament of ministry, the essential pattern of eucharistic worship on the Lord's Day, the classic shape of the liturgy freed from medieval and Reformation accretions, and the sense that participation in the liturgy has profound implications for the life of Christians in society.

It was clear that the prayer book tradition of Elizabeth and Cranmer was no longer adequate to speak to the realities of a church in modern American society. This realization had been implicit in the action of the 1928 General Convention when it established the Standing Liturgical Commission; it became explicit when the General Convention of 1964 called for a plan for trial usage of a proposed revision of the prayer book.

The plan adopted by General Convention was like no other revision process before it. It involved roughly three hundred consultants and writers who worked with the members of the Standing Liturgical Commission to reconsider every section of the prayer book. Over the course of six years, from 1967 to 1973, the commission published three books of liturgies for trial use: *The Liturgy of the Lord's Supper* in 1967, *Services for Trial Use* in 1970 (known as "The Green Book"), and *Authorized Services* in 1973 ("The Zebra Book"). As the trial liturgies were used in parishes throughout the church their reactions and responses, suggestions and criticisms were collected and considered. One of the outcomes of this process of trial use and feedback was the decision to include versions of the daily offices and the eucharist in both contemporary and Elizabethan English—Rite I and Rite II—because one single form of the liturgy was no longer going to be sufficient.

The sudden appearance of paperbound versions of what looked like a radically altered prayer book shocked people who had not been prepared for it. The options within services and the layout of the books themselves were confusing and unsettling after the fixed format of the 1928 book. I remember a conversation I had with a long-time member of the parish I attended as a college student. He was telling a group of us students about the history of the parish when he reached into a pew and held up a copy of "The Zebra Book" and solemnly declared, "This, ladies and gentlemen, is the book that will finally destroy the church."

Objections notwithstanding, in general the trial liturgies were thoughtfully received and used throughout the church . . . and they did not destroy it, after all. *The Draft Proposed Book of Common Prayer* was approved by the 1976 General Convention in Minneapolis by eighty- and ninety-percent majorities of lay and clergy representatives in the House of Deputies and by a nearly unanimous vote in the House of Bishops. By that vote it became *The Proposed Book of Common Prayer* with no further revisions and waited only to be approved by a simple yes or no vote at the 1979 convention. At that General Convention, meeting in Denver, *The Proposed Book of Common Prayer* was given nearly unanimous approval by both the House of Deputies and the House of Bishops and so became the official liturgy of the Episcopal Church.

In his book *The Anglican Vision*, James Griffiss states that the 1979 prayer book has opened the way for us to "understand more deeply that the Incarnation expresses our belief about the relationship between God and our humanity, and that the sacramental life is the living out of that relationship in the church and in the world."[15] Overall, the 1979 prayer book has moved worship in the Episcopal Church from being an experience primarily of text to one of liturgical actions. In other words, the congregation participates to a degree we have never known before; we are not simply listening to the priest, but together with the one who presides we are the doers of the liturgical action. Thus these actions can become vehicles for the activity of God in shaping and reshaping the community of believers. And so it is to the actions that make up the liturgies of the prayer book that we now turn.

Chapter 5

A Baptismal Church

If you pick up a prayer book in virtually any Episcopal Church and turn it on its side to look at the edge of the pages, one of the first things you may notice is a section about two-thirds of the way into the book marked by a narrow band of well-worn edges. Those pages are typically the section of the prayer book containing the rites for the Holy Eucharist, the part of the book regular worshipers know more or less by heart. But there is much more to the prayer book than those pages. Taken as a whole, the prayer book offers not just forms for public worship but a pattern for the Christian life, a way to discover what it means to be the body of Christ in the world. This chapter begins a "guided tour" of *The Book of Common Prayer,* so the best way to read this and the following chapter is with a prayer book ready at hand.

I remember as a teenager sitting in an inquirers' class in our parish rector's study and being taught (among many other details) that the church year begins not in January, but with the first Sunday of

Advent. I no longer believe that . . . exactly. I now believe that the church year begins, ends, and is reborn each year in the Easter waters of baptism. At the heart of the prayer book stands the liturgical celebration of Christ's death and resurrection—the paschal mystery—and our participation in that mystery through baptism and eucharist. The most significant feature of the 1979 prayer book, in fact, is the recovery of the ancient pattern of the church's keeping of the Passover of Christ. The celebration of this central event of the Christian faith is focused especially in the prayer book rites provided for the observance of Maundy Thursday, Good Friday, and the Great Vigil of Easter.

In the early church *every* Sunday was a celebration of the Easter event. The word "passover"—*pesach* in Hebrew, *pascha* in Greek—came to mean not only the Jewish festival commemorating God's saving of Israel from slavery in Egypt, but also the saving action of God in Jesus Christ, freeing us from the power of sin and death. Since Jesus rose from the dead on the first day of the week, among Christians every Lord's Day became a celebration of the Christian Passover. They called this first day of the week "The Eighth Day": in the death and resurrection of Christ, God had acted to make all creation new—an eighth day. Many baptismal fonts have been designed with eight sides, a visual memory of the deep associations between baptism and the eighth day. In the waters of baptism we enter the eighth day, we become new creations in Christ.

The liturgy for Holy Baptism directly follows that for the Great Vigil of Easter in the prayer book. The placement is not accidental. While the church in the first century kept only its weekly Day of the Lord, by the end of the second century the observance of a "Great Sunday" had emerged. This Sunday was the Lord's Day nearest to the date of Passover, and on this day an intensified celebration of the mystery of our participation in the death and resurrection of Christ was held. This Christian observance of Christ's death and resurrection, known as *Pascha*, became the premier occasion for the celebration of baptisms. Here are the roots of our celebration of Easter, and here we find the rationale for placing baptism and the Easter Vigil together in the prayer book.

Although baptism is entirely appropriate on other Sundays and feast days, especially All Saints' Day, the Feast of the Baptism of our Lord, Pentecost, and at the visitation of the bishop (see BCP 312), the meaning of baptism depends on Easter and is revealed most fully when baptism is celebrated in the context of the Easter Vigil. Even when there are no candidates for baptism, the prayer book provides a renewal of baptismal vows at the heart of the Easter Vigil. This renewal of vows may also be used on the other days for baptisms, and the connection to baptism is made explicit in the celebrant's words introducing the vows: "Through the Paschal mystery, dear friends, we are buried with Christ by Baptism into his death, and raised with him to newness of life" (BCP 292). It is this participation in the paschal mystery through baptism and eucharist that is the heart of the prayer book, and so we begin our tour with the liturgies of the *Triduum*.

∾ The Three Days of Easter

If we turn to the section of the prayer book called Proper Liturgies for Special Days (BCP 263), we will find the liturgies for the observance of Lent and the Three Days of Easter, the central focus of the liturgical year. Originally, the once-a-year celebration of Easter was a liturgical encounter with Christ's death *and* resurrection in a single act of worship. Over time, however, this unified celebration was expanded to include the days immediately preceding Easter. This was at least partially the result of a certain tendency to historicize the liturgy. Especially in Jerusalem, where Christians could and did gather at the traditional sites of major events in the passion story, forms of liturgical prayer developed to commemorate these events.

A definite pattern eventually emerged, and the mystery of Christ's passion, death, and resurrection was celebrated as a three-day liturgy that began at sundown on Thursday (the beginning of the Jewish day), extended through Friday and Saturday, and concluded at sundown on Easter Day. This pattern allowed for a fuller development of ritual and prayer and the final intensive preparation of candidates for baptism. In fact, the whole complex of services over these three days can be seen as an unfolding of the implications of baptism—our participation in the saving death and resurrection of Jesus Christ. The 1979 *Book of Common Prayer* has provided contemporary versions of the ancient liturgies of these three days, which are characterized by a solemn simplicity and a rich use of symbol.

～ *Maundy Thursday*

The Three Days of the Christian Passover begin with a simple familiarity; the rubric opening the liturgy for Maundy Thursday directs: "The Eucharist begins in the usual manner" (BCP 274). On this night we share the meal that Jesus filled with the meaning of his death and resurrection, the meal that reconstitutes the church in that same paschal mystery week by week. The eucharist is a fundamental means by which we are incorporated into the dying and rising of Christ, by which we renew our baptismal identity.

The meaning of that identity in Christ is expressed in additional ritual actions on this night. The Maundy Thursday celebration allows for the ceremony of foot washing—from which the day actually takes its name. In Latin the word "commandment" is *mandatum*. At the last supper Jesus says to his disciples, "I give you a new commandment, that you love one another" (John 13:34). Jesus takes the role of a servant by washing the disciples' feet, revealing his identity as servant of all; servanthood was to be the sign of those who follow him. The washing of feet is meant to be a ritual identification with the servanthood of Christ, a declaration of who we are by baptism. At one time another mark of the liturgy of this day—expressing the same identification with Christ's servanthood—was a special collection of gifts for the poor. Those who have been fed at the table of the Lord must become food for others.

～ *Good Friday*

The Good Friday liturgy includes the proclamation of the passion from the gospel of John, an ancient elaborated form of the prayers of the people, and provision for devotions before a wooden cross. Holy Communion may be administered from the sacrament reserved from the celebration of the previous evening. The service has no formal entrance rite and no blessing or dismissal: since the church began its *Triduum* celebration on Thursday evening, the Good Friday liturgy is simply a gathering together for a focused offering of prayer at a particular moment in the course of the three days. A friend once suggested to me that another way to look at the services of these three days is as one extended liturgy with several long intermissions!

Devotions before the cross—sometimes called the veneration of the cross—can be misleading as to the overall intent and spirit of these days. I remember in my youth walking into church on Good Friday to see the crucifix on the altar draped in black. The hymns struck my ears as mournful, their tone sounded grief-stricken:

> O sorrow deep! Who would not weep
>   with heartfelt pain and sighing!
> God the Father's only Son
>   in the tomb is lying.[1]

Other Anglicans may remember three-hour devotions on Good Friday, with preaching on the "Seven Last Words" Jesus said from the cross. (This service, incidentally, seems to have originated in Jesuit preaching missions of the seventeenth century.) In whatever form they take, the implication of many Good Friday services is that on this Friday we gather to mourn, to recreate or remember the crucifixion, the death of Christ.

However, mourning is not the intent of the prayer book's Good Friday liturgy. We do not bring a wooden cross into our assembly in order to mourn a dead Jesus. Jesus Christ is alive. The purpose of our gathering is not to recreate sacred history, but to worship a living Lord. The cross is venerated as the sign of the victory of Christ, the sign we receive in baptism. Look at the first anthem provided to be sung with the cross in view:

> We glory in your cross, O Lord,
> and praise and glorify your holy resurrection;
> for by virtue of your cross
> joy has come to the whole world. (BCP 281)

The Good Friday liturgy—indeed all the liturgies of these three days—is not meant to entertain us or even edify us, but to involve us, to draw us into the mystery of Christ's death and resurrection as a present reality. The words of Ezra Pound to fledgling poets is true of the intent of these celebrations: "Do not describe, present."

～ The Great Vigil of Easter

The Great Vigil of Easter makes it clear that the liturgies of these three days truly are encounters with the living Christ. The 1979 *Book of Common Prayer* is the first prayer book to include the Easter Vigil; before the 1970s it was experienced only in seminary chapels or a few isolated parishes. In the ancient church, however, it was the most significant liturgy of the year and its recovery is central to our understanding of what the liturgical year *is*. If the liturgical life of the church is an encounter with the death and resurrection of Christ, then our sacramental celebrations are the means of our incorporation into that mystery. In other words, they make real our participation in the dying and rising body of Christ in the world. The Easter Vigil is the occasion for that participation *par excellence*.

The liturgy begins in darkness with the celebrant's address to the people:

> Dear friends in Christ: On this most holy night, in which our Lord Jesus passed over from death to life, the Church invites her members, dispersed throughout the world, to gather in vigil and prayer. For this is the Passover of the Lord, in which, by hearing his Word and celebrating his Sacraments, we share in his victory over death. (BCP 285)

This—this night, this service, this moment—is the Passover of the Lord, as the deacon will then sing repeatedly in the *Exsultet*. What we gather to celebrate in the Easter Vigil is not a fond reminiscence, but a present reality. We gather to participate in the death and resurrection of Christ, principally in the baptism of new members of Christ's body, but also in the renewal of all the baptized.

The Easter Vigil has four parts: the service of light, the scripture readings, Christian initiation, and the Holy Eucharist. This is only a bare outline for a service of many layers of symbol and meaning. The Great Vigil of Easter presents the mystery of the resurrection in the elemental language of creation itself: darkness, light, fire, smoke, wax, water, oil, touch, words, bread, wine. In the darkness a light is kindled and blessed. The paschal candle is lighted and carried in procession before the people, representing the pillar of cloud and fire that led Israel in the wilderness. Members of the congregation may hold smaller candles that are lighted from the paschal candle. The deacon leads the *Exsultet*, the ancient blessing of God for the mighty act of salvation in the resurrection of Christ.

Then follows a series of readings, the story of salvation history. The prayer book provides nine lessons and directs that at least two of them must be read, including the story of Israel's deliverance at the Red Sea in Exodus. The readings *are* the vigil: a lengthy series of readings is the heart of a liturgical vigil, usually interspersed with psalms, canticles, and prayers, as they are on this night. After the telling of the story of salvation, new members are added to the ongoing story of God's people in the celebration of Holy Baptism. In the absence of candidates for baptism, the renewal of baptismal vows takes place. Following baptism and its renewal, the Easter eucharist is celebrated, beginning with the proclamation of what we have just experienced sacramentally: Alleluia. Christ is risen!

～ Holy Baptism

The liturgical scholar Marion Hatchett observes that in most cultures "initiation is the central liturgy of the community"; in other words, the rites of initiation serve as models for all the other major rites of a particular church or community.[2] Even though the majority of baptisms in most churches are still celebrated at times other than the Great Vigil of Easter, in congregations where the vigil is celebrated in its fullness year after year, every baptism will vibrate with images of the church gathered on the night of Christ's Passover.

In our celebration of Holy Baptism we declare all that is most significant about our identity—it is, after all, the means by which we become who we are as members of the body of Christ. The rite for the celebration of baptism in the 1979 *Book of Common Prayer* represents a deep shift in the consciousness of what it means to be church, a shift initiated by the biblical and liturgical movements of this century. Likewise, earlier rites for Christian initiation in Anglicanism reflected the self-understanding of the church of their own times.

If you think of Clarence Day's autobiographical *Life with Father*, for example, you will see a humorous picture of the Episcopal Church in upper-class American life at the turn of the century. It is suddenly discovered that through some oversight the respectable patriarch of the family was never baptized. This vaguely embarrassing discovery has to be rectified; Father is spirited off to an Episcopal church in the suburbs for a quick and very private service of baptism. Here is a picture of baptism as a social rite of passage, rather like attending the correct schools. *The Book of Common Prayer* that would have been used for the father's baptism included only a single mention in a prayer that baptism was a sharing in the death and resurrection of Christ. Since it assumed that the ordinary candidate for baptism would be an infant, the confession of faith was reduced to a summary question: "Dost thou believe all the articles of the Christian faith as contained in the Apostles' Creed?"

In much the same way, the 1979 *Book of Common Prayer* reflects our current understanding of baptism—now as the central rite of the entire worshiping community. The instructions concerning baptism note this change: "Holy Baptism is appropriately administered within the Eucharist as the chief service on a Sunday or other feast" (BCP 298). Earlier editions of the prayer book directed that baptisms take place after the second reading at Morning or Evening Prayer or at other "convenient" times. In practice, this meant in many cases that baptism was celebrated in private, with only parents, godparents, family, and friends in attendance.

A mother of two college-age children once said to me, "I can't believe you require parents and godparents to attend classes. When my kids were baptized all I had to do was get their christening gowns on and show up on Saturday afternoon." The whole congregation now regularly experiences the celebration of baptism, and this experience has begun to challenge many assumptions about just what we mean by this sacrament. With the inclusion of the renewal of baptismal vows, the experience is no longer merely a private social rite of passage, but a renewal of adult commitment and communal responsibility.

The rite for Holy Baptism assumes that the *normative* candidate for baptism is an adult.[3] Without denying the importance of baptizing the children of adult believers, the fullest expression of the meaning of the rite is seen in the consciously chosen decision of an adult believer to enter the baptized life, as is made clear in the service by the presentation of adult candidates first. Children are baptized on the basis of the faith of the adults who present them, with the clear expectation that they will be raised in the context of that adult faith with every opportunity to make it their own. After the presentation the candidates then join in a renunciation of Satan, "the evil powers of this world," and "all sinful desires"—a version of the ancient renunciations—and make three corresponding declarations of adherence to Jesus Christ as savior, with the promise to follow and obey Christ as Lord. In response the entire congregation promises to support the newly baptized in their new life in Christ and then joins with the candidates in confessing their faith in God as Father, Son, and Holy Spirit in the Baptismal Covenant.

The Baptismal Covenant is a combination of an ancient question-and-answer version of the Apostles' Creed and what might be called "So what?" questions—questions that draw out the implications of the faith professed in the creed. "Will you continue in the apostles' teaching and fellowship ...? Will you persevere in resisting evil ...? Will you proclaim by word and example the Good News ...? Will you seek and serve Christ in all persons ...? Will you strive for justice and peace ...?" (BCP 304–305). The Baptismal Covenant says that faith is not simply a matter of giving intellectual assent to a series of propositions about God, but is a matter of lifestyle, behaviors, and concrete commitments.

The covenant is followed by a series of intercessions for those to be baptized, praying that God will do for them what we have just promised ourselves to do. The celebrant then blesses the water of baptism, giving thanks in a prayer rich with references to the water of creation, the saving passage of Israel through the sea, the baptism of Jesus, and the passing over of Jesus from death to resurrection. It makes clear our own sharing in that death and rebirth by the water of baptism.

If the bishop is presiding at the celebration, the oil of chrism may also be blessed. The anointing of newly baptized persons has a long and complicated history in the church.[4] Although it was retained in the 1549 prayer book, from the revision of 1552 on the anointing with oil, or chrismation, officially disappeared from Anglican practice, not appearing in *The Book of Common Prayer* in any subsequent revision until the 1979 prayer book. Its use, however, has rich biblical connotations and the word *chrism* is related to the word *christen*, to "en-Christ." Several of our titles for Jesus himself are rooted in this practice of anointing: *Christos* is simply the Greek word for "Anointed One," which is *Messiah* in Hebrew. The anointing makes ritually explicit what the sacrament of baptism intends: rebirth into the image and likeness of Christ, that the newly baptized might "share in the royal priesthood of Jesus Christ" (BCP 307).

The baptism in water follows. The words accompanying the washing in water are based on Matthew 28:19: "Go therefore and make disciples of all nations, baptizing them in the name of the Father and of the Son and of the Holy Spirit." The earliest Christian practice of baptism involved a triple affirmation of faith accompanied by threefold immersion in water.

Over time the creeds developed from these baptismal forms, but the simpler statement of Matthew remained as a baptismal formula, a succinct statement of the faith.

Note the rubric about baptism by water: "Each candidate is presented by name to the Celebrant, . . . who then immerses, or pours water upon, the candidate" (BCP 307). The word Greek word *baptizein* means "to dip." Immersion in water is the oldest baptismal practice of the church. By the middle ages the pouring of water, or affusion, had become customary in some places, but a generous use of water remained the official preference. The 1549 prayer book called for a triple immersion "discreetly and warily done." And the rubrics of the 1662 prayer book read thus:

> (If they certify that the Child may well endure it) he shall dip it in the Water discreetly and warily.... But if they certify that the Child is week, it shall suffice to pour Water upon it.

The first American prayer book likewise directed that the child should be dipped in water or that the water should be poured. In the 1979 book the word "dip" has simply been changed to "immerse." The practice of immersion—either of infants or adults—is not the ordinary experience today of most Anglicans, although attempts to recover the use of ample amounts of water are being made in more and more places. It is difficult to say why the practice of the sacrament of new birth has been reduced to droplets of water flung from a small bowl onto the forehead of a baby, but that kind of sacramental minimalism is clearly not what the prayer book intends. A later

chapter will have more to say about the stewardship
of sacramental signs.

Finally, the newly baptized person is signed with
the cross (with the optional use of chrism) and is formally welcomed into the full communion of the
church with the words "We receive you into the
household of God" (BCP 308). The peace is exchanged
and the service continues with the prayers of the people or the offertory of the eucharist.

～ Confirmation

Immediately following the service of baptism are the
rites for confirmation, reception, and reaffirmation.
The history of confirmation is related in some ways to
the history of baptismal anointing, but it is even more
complex. Originally, baptism meant a series of stages
and ritual actions: catechesis, preparation by prayer
and fasting, the water bath, post-baptismal laying on
of hands and anointing, and first communion. Over
time, these unified events constituting initiation into
the church were separated into discreet parts. Some,
like the catechumenate, were lost altogether, while
others took on a significance of their own.
Confirmation is one of those events. Its roots are in the
laying on of hands and anointing that followed baptism, but by the middle ages it had become a separate
rite celebrated by the bishop when he arrived.[5]

In the 1979 prayer book an attempt has been made
to restore the original sense of the laying on of hands
and anointing as integral to the celebration of baptism. The prayer that immediately follows the immersion in water, "Heavenly Father, we thank you that by
water and the Holy Spirit you have bestowed..."

(BCP 308), is a reworking of the prayer that was said at the separate service called Confirmation in earlier prayer books. It is now said by the priest or bishop over every newly baptized person and is accompanied (either before or after) by the laying on of hands in the act of signing with the cross and chrismation.

What the prayer book now calls confirmation is intended to be a mature public affirmation of baptismal faith. When that affirmation is made by someone who has already made a mature public profession of faith in another church and who now wishes to live out that faith in the Episcopal Church, the rite is called Reception, and when an already confirmed Episcopalian—for whatever reason—chooses to make a formal recommitment of faith, it is called reaffirmation.

The rite for Holy Baptism concludes with a section of Additional Directions. These often overlooked directions for variations in the service also provide clarifications and suggestions for ritual actions, such as the giving of a baptismal candle.

As we have seen, in the early church receiving the bread and wine of the eucharist was the culmination of the whole sequence of events that made up Christian initiation. What we call baptism ordinarily included and reached its climax in the reception of communion—those who had been made members of the body of Christ were now welcomed to receive the sacrament of their own identity. A recovery of this essential linkage between baptism and eucharist has led to the growing practice in the Episcopal Church of giving infants Holy Communion from the time of their baptism. As one Anglican report puts it, we have begun to realize that it "is paradoxical to admit children to membership in the body of Christ through baptism, and yet to deny that membership in the eucharistic meal that follows."[6] Every celebration of the eucharist is a celebration of the identity we have received in baptism as the body of Christ. It is to the eucharist and the prayer book's pattern for living out the eucharistic life that we now turn.

Chapter 6

The Eucharist and Daily Office

D oing communion is complicated!" a twelve-year-old acolyte once exclaimed to me after her first training session with the deacon. At one level the prayer book celebration of the Holy Eucharist is very simple: clergy and people gather, scriptures are read, a sermon is preached, prayer is offered, bread and wine are brought to the table, thanks is given to God, the meal is shared, and the people depart. This pattern has been described in some detail as early as the second century.

In most Anglican prayer books this simplicity has carried through in the sense of having a single liturgy for the eucharist, although it has often been cloaked in lengthy texts and elaborate language. Officially at least, all worshipers had to do was open the book to the page on which the order for Holy Communion began and follow it through to the end. For Anglicans around the world today, however, it is no longer that easy. Even churches that officially use the 1662 prayer book have a variety of eucharistic liturgies available to them. Similarly, the 1979 *Book of Common Prayer* provides a number of options and resources for celebrating the Holy Eucharist in different ways. In addition to the two rites for the eucharist, for example, there are six versions of the prayers of the people (with provision for congregations to adapt and create their own) and eight eucharistic prayers.

As we have seen, this provision for variety and flexibility is a response to the changing needs and circumstances of contemporary worshipers. The prayer book tradition has evolved to allow and encourage congregations to shape worship according to local circumstances, to meet local pastoral, evangelistic, and liturgical needs. But simply thumbing through the wealth of material on the eucharist in the prayer book can be bewildering. Congregations typically settle into their own patterns, so long-standing members usually have little trouble navigating the pages for the texts they need. But it may be quite a different story for newcomers. Even carefully crafted bulletins and worship booklets often do little to help the worshiper through what can seem like a maze.

Still, whether the celebration is conducted according to Rite I or Rite II, whether it includes every option or only a few, whether its ceremonial is elaborate or austere, eucharists celebrated according to the 1979 prayer book share a fundamental pattern. And knowing that pattern is the best way to understand the nature of the rite we celebrate.

Liturgy is not simply words on a page; rather, each liturgy has a unique shape.[1] The simplest way to describe the shape of the eucharistic liturgy is to name its two principal parts: Word and Meal. The 1979 *Book of Common Prayer* provides a convenient outline of that shape in the final form provided for the celebration of the eucharist, An Order for Celebrating the Holy Eucharist (BCP 400). Sometimes referred to as "Rite III," this form is intended for occasional, informal celebrations of the eucharist. It is simply a guideline for congregations who wish to craft liturgies for particular occasions. But the major headings of that outline can serve to guide our reflections here on the structure undergirding the variations for celebrating the eucharist in the prayer book.

In the prayer book small words can be very important. Words like "may" or "shall" in the rubrics can indicate big changes in terms of what the celebration will look and feel like. For instance, in Rite I the rubric says that "the Celebrant *may* say" the opening acclamation, "Blessed be God," making it is possible to begin the eucharist right off with the Collect for Purity, just as in the 1928 book and earlier versions. Flexibility on this particular point is not given in Rite II, where the word "may" does not appear in the corresponding rubric. So as we consider the shape of the eucharist in the prayer book we need to pay attention to the rubrics in italics, and especially to the small words that indicate big changes.

∾ Gathering in the Lord's Name

There was an uproar in a parish I know when the buildings and grounds committee decided to take up the carpet in the church and refinish the hardwood floors. The primary objection was the noise level. "You can hear everybody's shoes when they're coming into church," said one man. "That's right," wrote the worship committee chairman in a letter of response. "The first act of the eucharist is when we gather."

There are many ways for the church to structure its gathering. Perhaps the most common first act of gathering is the singing of a hymn while clergy, choir, and other ministers enter in procession—but it should be noted that a processional hymn is simply one option. The presider then begins an acclamation appropriate to the liturgical season: "Blessed be God...," or "Alleluia. Christ is risen," or "Bless the Lord who forgives all our sins." The function of this acclamation is to declare in whose name we gather. Prayers and songs of praise or petition follow.

The collect of the day concludes the entrance rite, this ritual of gathering. This opening prayer of the liturgy does what its name implies: it collects or gathers the prayers of the individuals who make up this particular assembly and brings them into a common act of prayer to the God who has gathered them. The classic three-part structure of a collect includes address to God, petition, and doxology. The language of an individual collect often contains images relating to a particular time in the liturgical year, but its primary purpose is not to announce a "theme" for the liturgy. The collect's purpose is to gather the prayer of a particular assembly into one corporate act.[2]

Consider, for example, the collect for the Second Sunday of Easter:

> Almighty and everlasting God, who in the Paschal mystery established the new covenant of reconciliation: Grant that all who have been reborn into the fellowship of Christ's Body may

show forth in their lives what they profess by their faith; through Jesus Christ our Lord, who lives and reigns with you and the Holy Spirit, one God, for ever and ever. *Amen.* (BCP 224)

While the themes of the Easter season are clearly present, the prayer makes use of them to ask God to accomplish something in the lives of those who are gathered here to pray. People come to the liturgy with all their individual concerns and life situations; the collect asks God to make of those individual lives one common witness.

∼ The Liturgy of the Word

Once the assembly has been gathered, its first action is to proclaim and respond to the word of God. And again, the prayer book provides a variety of ways for this to take place. The pattern of proclamation and response might include scripture reading, silence, song, sermon, profession of faith, prayer, reconciliation, and the peace.

Both Rite I and Rite II direct that one or two lessons be read before the gospel. The earliest Christians naturally read only from the Hebrew scriptures, but added specifically Christian readings as they became available; in fact, the gospels were written precisely for this liturgical purpose. The number of readings varied widely, but a classic pattern of three readings emerged eventually: Old Testament, New Testament, and gospel. In the medieval period the number of readings was reduced to two in most places, so that readings from the Hebrew scriptures were rarely heard in the Sunday eucharistic liturgy. This is the pattern Cranmer's prayer book inherited and the pattern of subsequent revisions until the present one.

The eucharistic lectionary in the 1979 prayer book is a version of the Roman Catholic lectionary prepared after the Second Vatican Council in consultation with scholars of other denominations, including Episcopalians. Versions of this lectionary are used by Lutherans, Presbyterians, Methodists, and others. The readings are arranged in a three-year cycle: Year A features the gospel of Matthew, Year B Mark, and Year C Luke. Three readings and a psalm are appointed for every Sunday and major feast day of the year. The rubrics in both Rite I and II note that silence and a psalm, hymn, or anthem may follow each reading.

The sermon is an integral part of the proclamation of the word of God in the liturgy. There is nothing in the prayer book to suggest that the sermon is optional. Nothing stands between the proclamation of the gospel reading and its explication in the sermon. The sermon is an extension of the proclamation of the scripture readings just heard. Its purpose is a sacramental one: to uncover how the history of salvation recorded in the Bible is the story of our own lives— how our lives reveal God's presence no less than the stories of scripture.

Originally, the eucharistic prayer was regarded as the church's profession of faith. Gradually, however, the Nicene Creed made its way into the liturgy, as the church sought to define and maintain its doctrinal formulations in the face of various heretical movements. Unlike some of the continental reformers, the drafters of the first *Book of Common Prayer* retained the Nicene Creed in the eucharist. There was, however, opposition to it in the first proposed book in the United States on the grounds that it contained "unscriptural phrases." The original form of this creed in the first-person plural is the basis for the translation provided in both Rite I and II. Rite I also contains the "I" form of the creed familiar to some from previous prayer books—"I believe in God" rather than "We believe." This "I" form originated in the period when the congregation had ceased to have any active role in the liturgy and the priest was left to say the texts alone. The creed is only required to be said on Sundays and major feasts.

Some form of the prayers of the people has followed the readings and sermon from at least the second century. One classic pattern from fourth- or fifth-century Rome is reflected in the Solemn Collects provided for Good Friday: a series of biddings, periods of silence, and collects. The prayer book now offers several options and models for offering the intercessions of the church. Rite I includes the prayer "for the whole state of Christ's Church and the world" (BCP 328), some version of which has appeared in every prayer book since 1549 (where it followed the *Sanctus*). The rubrics for Rite I direct that prayer be offered according to this form or following the directions for the prayers of the people found on page 383.

In that section six forms of intercessory prayer are provided. These forms may be used as printed, or adapted to local needs. Forms I and V are extended litanies, Form IV a somewhat shorter litany, Forms III and VI have variable congregational responses, and Form II takes the form of a bidding prayer. Whatever form they take the intercessions must include the categories listed at the top of page 383. Although the forms provided are intended to be models for the creation of prayers addressing local concerns, and not necessarily used verbatim, it is quite common to hear a leader of prayer announce, "This morning we will use Form IV of the prayers of the people," and then ask people to turn to such and such a page in the prayer book. This is one of those places where the small words make a big difference: the rubrics on page 383 include the word "may" many times, and indeed the rubrics clearly state that "adaptations or insertions suitable to the occasion may be made."[3]

Following the prayers of the people, provision is made in both Rite I and II for a confession of sin to take place before the peace "if it has not been said earlier" (BCP 359), as it might have been if the Penitential Order opened the service. The rubrics further indicate that the general confession may be omitted "on occasion," as is appropriate, for example, during the Great Fifty Days of Easter. The general confession was introduced into the eucharist at the time of the Reformation; the ancient sign of reconciliation in the liturgy was not confession and absolution, but the sharing of the kiss of peace. Those who had need of repentance did so before they came to the eucharist.

The Exhortation advises those who need help in their examination of conscience to go "to a discreet and understanding priest, and confess your sins, that you may receive the benefit of absolution, and spiritual counsel and advice" (BCP 317). For this purpose the prayer book provides two forms for The Reconciliation of a Penitent. Furthermore, the Disciplinary Rubrics give directions for dealing with individuals who refuse to repent of some known sin or who refuse to be reconciled with their neighbor (BCP 409). The traditional Christian understanding of the public implications of sin and reconciliation is reflected in these rubrics.

Exchanging a sign of peace at this point in the eucharist is the ancient conclusion to the Liturgy of the Word. Some scholars find evidence of this liturgical action in the New Testament itself (see, for example 1 Corinthians 16:20, or 1 Peter 5:14). The peace disappeared from the prayer book after 1549 until the present revision. Celebrant and people greet one another formally, and the rubric directs that all the ministers and people may greet one another "in the name of the Lord," standing reconciled and ready to offer the gifts of the eucharistic meal.

∽ The Holy Communion

The eucharistic action can be described as having a fourfold shape: bread and wine are prepared, blessed, broken, and given. This way of understanding the meal stands behind all the options and variations offered in the prayer book for celebrating this part of the eucharist.

∽ *Preparation*

In the early church, the bread and wine for the eucharist were offered by members of the congregation, each of whom brought the bread and wine they would need for the service—thus the designation of this action as the "offertory." Today the bread and wine are usually provided by the altar guild, but the offertory is still largely a practical matter. Bread and wine, together with money and other gifts, are collected and the table is made ready. The bread and wine are to be brought directly to the deacon or priest and placed on the altar.

~ *Blessing*

The prayer book calls the eucharistic prayer The Great Thanksgiving. The Greek word *eucharistia* means thanksgiving. Christian eucharistic prayers derive from the prayer of thanksgiving said over the final cup of wine at formal Jewish meals. The classic shape of these prayers includes a dialogue establishing the corporate nature of the prayer ("Let us give thanks" ... "It is right to do so"), the blessing of God for the gift of creation and redemption (typically in the form of a rehearsal of salvation history), and supplication that God will continue to show mercy to the faithful in the present day. The prayer concludes with the corporate act of assent to what has been prayed, "Amen."

The 1979 prayer book provides two eucharistic prayers in Rite I and four in Rite II. In addition, there are two forms that allow the celebrant to offer praise in his or her own words (BCP 402, 404). Eucharistic Prayer I in Rite I is the prayer found in every American prayer book since 1789. It focuses on the sacrifice of Christ and departs from ancient tradition in that it contains no praise of God for creation. Eucharistic Prayer II is a revision of Prayer I with a greater emphasis on the gift of creation and the incarnation of Christ.

In Rite II, Eucharistic Prayer A translates into contemporary language the traditional Anglican emphasis in the eucharist on the cross of Christ. Prayer B is a reworking of one of the earliest eucharistic prayers known to us, the eucharistic prayer of the third-century Roman bishop Hippolytus. The focus of Prayer B is the role of God's Word in the creation and salvation of the world in Christ. Prayer C is a modern composition emphasizing the revelation of God in and through creation. It is somewhat penitential in tone and features variable congregational responses throughout the prayer. Eucharist Prayer D is a version of the fourth-century prayer of St. Basil. This prayer is in use among Eastern Orthodox Christians, and versions of it are now authorized in the Roman Catholic, Anglican, Methodist, and Lutheran churches. Prayer D encompasses the classic themes of all the other eucharistic prayers and is the prayer with the greatest historical and ecumenical significance.

The eucharistic prayer is a unity from the opening dialogue (sometimes called the *Sursum Corda*, "Lift up your hearts") through the Amen and Our Father. Nevertheless, within the structure of the prayer variations occur, such as the inclusion of proper prefaces. The *Sanctus*, which has been included consistently in eucharistic prayers since the fourth or fifth century, is only one acclamation assigned to the people and is sung to a great variety of settings. All four prayers of Rite II contain different congregational acclamations in the prayer after the *Sanctus*, and every eucharistic prayer concludes with the necessary congregational Amen.

～ *Breaking*

Although like the preparation of gifts it is an essentially practical action (bread must be broken in order to be shared and eaten), every Anglican prayer book from the first has remembered the ritual importance of breaking the bread into pieces. Even when the bread is made up of individual wafers, the significance of breaking at least representative pieces of it has been maintained as a sign of the unity of the church. Many congregations today are using loaf bread as a more eloquent sign of the one body of Christ in which we all share.

After the consecrated bread is broken the rubrics direct that a period of silence is to be kept. Then may follow an anthem, called the Fraction Anthem. The prayer book provides a number of alternative texts: Christ our Passover is printed in both Rite I and II. Rite I also includes for the first time in an American prayer book the *Agnus Dei,* "O Lamb of God." An anthem may be sung, or the entire action take place in silence. The pre-communion devotional Prayer of Humble Access has appeared in various forms and in various places in Anglican eucharistic rites; its use is optional in Rite I.

～ *Giving*

Holy Communion is received by the ministers and people in both kinds, bread and wine. At the time of communion in the liturgy congregations tend to rely on unnecessary but established customs and norms and it is instructive to note what the prayer book does *not* say about the reception of communion. The ancient practice of the church was to receive communion standing, a posture that emphasizes the understanding that because Christ has saved us we are worthy to stand before God. It was not until later in the middle ages that the custom of kneeling became widespread. Both postures have been observed in Anglican history and the 1979 prayer book makes no mention of either at the time of communion.

Altar rails were introduced in the early seventeenth century to prevent dogs from fouling the altar. It was not until sometime later that these became "communion rails" at which people knelt for communion, and their use has never been indicated by rubric in a prayer book. Well into the eighteenth century, the ministers of communion moved out into the congregation to administer the sacrament.[4] The 1979 prayer book makes no mention of the place of reception, only that the bishops, priests, and deacons receive "while the people are coming forward" (BCP 407).

After receiving communion, the congregation gives thanks and receives a blessing. The 1979 prayer book has restored a feature that was originally much more significant than a priestly blessing, the dismissal. Having renewed their baptismal identity as the servant body of Christ, the people are sent out in peace to "love and serve the Lord" (BCP 340/366). So that nothing will detract from the plain meaning of this dismissal to go out to "do the work you have given us to do" (BCP 366), it should be noted that—contrary to common practice—the prayer book does not authorize even a hymn to be sung after the dismissal.

∽ The Daily Office

If the heart of the prayer book is the celebration of the paschal mystery of Christ in baptism and eucharist, then its soul may be the daily office. Christian identity is given and renewed in the celebration of baptism and eucharist; it is lived out and shaped by daily prayer and the call to various ways of life in the world. *The Book of Common Prayer* gives liturgical voice to these realities in a section titled The Daily Office, with liturgies for prayer in the morning, noon, evening, and night, and suggestions for daily devotions.

One of the principal gifts to Anglicanism in the first *Book of Common Prayer* was the simplification of the medieval monastic tradition of daily prayer and the restoration of a vision of daily prayer as the work of the whole church, not just the clergy or monastic elite. Having said that, it is true that versions of the daily office in all subsequent prayer books, including 1979, are still heavily influenced by the monastic tradition, though simplified and adapted for the use of groups and individuals living active lives in the world.

A few years ago the superior of the Society of St. John the Evangelist, Martin L. Smith, wrote in *Episcopal Life* of the popularity of monastic guest houses. Large numbers of people, he said, seem to be drawn to share the life of monastic communities for a time. He described the attraction of the "monastic impulse" by telling of a woman he knew whose daily practice was to watch the six o'clock news, have a drink, and read evening prayer on her patio. This is an example of monastic spirituality, said Smith, because it is completely ordinary and does not depend on how she happens to feel at any given moment.

Daily prayer in the prayer book tradition embodies a spiritual practice that is practical, ordered, and not dependent on feelings that are subject to change. The daily offices of the prayer book are intended to be familiar, regular, and participatory, leading to what one author calls a "divine monotony."[5] Indeed, the word "office" is derived from the Latin *officium*, meaning the performance of a task or duty. The offices have a corporate familiarity that leads us deeper into the regular rhythms of the day and of our life with God. Whether said alone or in small groups or sung in a large gathering, the daily office is the common prayer of the church. Over time, faithful participation in this daily prayer can form a spirituality that is balanced, grounded in scripture, and genuinely corporate. In the parish I now serve the staff gathers morning and evening to sing the daily office. That usually means just three or four of us, but even when I find myself alone for some reason at the appointed time, I am aware that I am part of an ongoing and daily community of prayer.

The psalms and scripture readings form the heart of the daily office. The daily praying of the psalms in particular—the ancient songbook of Jews and Christians, filled with their devastatingly honest blessings and cursings—can act as an antidote to the subjectivity and individualization of our culture. As Kathleen Norris writes in her book on the monastic impulse, *The Cloister Walk*, the psalter "counters our tendency to see individual experience as sufficient for formulating a vision of the world."[6]

Historically, psalms and scripture readings form the main body of the daily office. In the 1979 prayer book this is the section from The Invitatory and Psalter through the collects. This section in both

Morning and Evening Prayer includes psalms, lessons, canticles, the Apostles' Creed, the Lord's Prayer, and versicles and responses. It resembles the medieval monastic offices out of which it grew and is essentially the shape of the daily office in the 1549 prayer book.

To the beginning of this main body of the daily office the prayer book of 1552 added a penitential beginning: an opening sentence and confession. And the prayer book of 1662 added a concluding section of additional prayers. A careful look at the rubrics reveals this three-part structure. For example, the instructions at the beginning of Morning Prayer indicate that the service begins with the opening sentence and what follows *or* directly with the versicle "Lord, open our lips" (BCP 75). Similarly, at the conclusion of the collects, the rubric reads that additional intercessions and thanksgivings *may* follow.

The earliest form of the church's daily liturgical prayer was characterized by a selective use of psalms appropriate to the time of day, short acclamations and antiphons, and the use of colorful ceremonial—the ritual lighting of lamps and the use of incense, for example. As daily prayer developed in the monasteries, it became increasingly elaborated and focused on the meditative recital of the entire psalter and other portions of scripture. This was the only approach to the daily office known to Archbishop Cranmer and the other Anglican reformers, who were concerned that the laity become thoroughly familiar with the contents of the Bible. The result was a daily office in which large quantities of scripture were recited and read. In Cranmer's first prayer book all one hundred fifty psalms were to be read in course monthly and the entire New Testament (with the exception of Revelation) three times during the year.

In its plan for the systematic reading of scripture, called a lectionary, the 1979 prayer book offers more flexibility than previous prayer books. The Daily Office Lectionary is a two-year cycle, with Year One beginning in Advent preceding odd-numbered years. With a few seasonal exceptions, the psalms are designed to be read in a seven-week cycle. The Old Testament is largely read through once over the course of the two years, and the New Testament twice.

The Psalter in the 1979 prayer book is a translation that takes into account current scholarship regarding the Hebrew text. It is also a liturgical psalter; that is, the psalms are arranged for the use of a worshiping assembly, and the cadences of the text lend themselves to singing or group recitation. The asterisk printed in the middle of verses indicates either a pause when the psalm is read or the conclusion of a musical phrase to which the psalm is being sung. If you look at Psalm 1 you will see the heading First Day: Morning Prayer; before Psalm 6 you will see First Day: Evening Prayer. Here the prayer book still provides for Cranmer's scheme of reading the psalter in a monthly cycle. The Latin titles at the start of each psalm are printed as an aid to research and to the wealth of historical musical settings of the psalms.

Two additional offices with readings and hymns are provided by the 1979 prayer book to mark the course of the day: An Order of Service for Noonday and An Order for Compline. The noonday office follows the traditional monastic pattern for minor offices during the day: Terce, Sext, and None, as they are called, or the "little offices." The psalms are those traditionally associated with these offices, and the prayers speak of the mission of the church and to events such as Christ hanging on the cross at this hour.

Compline has become one of the most popular services of the church, especially at conferences and in small gatherings. Its roots can be traced as early as the fourth century, when it was the bedtime prayer of monks. Again, the psalms are those traditionally associated with this office: *The Rule of St. Benedict* specifies the reading of Psalms 4, 91, and 134, which are included here. The prayers ask for God's protection "through the hours of this night," and the office concludes with the Song of Simeon with its antiphon: "Guide us waking, O Lord, and guard us sleeping; that awake we may watch with Christ, and asleep we may rest in peace."

Also new to the 1979 prayer book is An Order of Worship for the Evening. This rich and variable form for prayer in the evening is a recovery of elements that can be traced to the third century, and thus represents a style of daily prayer that predates the development of the monastic type of office. In the next chapter we will use An Order of Worship for the Evening to demonstrate how the prayer book can be a resource for pastoral liturgy.

Finally, the section of the prayer book on the daily office concludes with Daily Devotions for Individuals and Families. These brief forms of prayer intended for use by individuals and families at home or work follow the basic structure of the daily offices. Their rubrics indicate how they may be expanded with appropriate canticles, hymns, the Apostles' Creed, and so forth, though their brevity makes them especially useful for people who wish to offer the daily prayer of the church in the midst of busy lives.

∿ Pastoral Offices

The section of the prayer book called Pastoral Offices includes rites of passage, rites of personal vocation, and rites marking significant life crises. They are presented in a natural order: Confirmation (when it is administered apart from baptism), A Form of Commitment to Christian Service, The Celebration and Blessing of a Marriage, A Thanksgiving for the Birth or Adoption of a Child, The Reconciliation of a Penitent, Ministration to the Sick, Ministration at the Time of Death, and The Burial of the Dead.

Underlying all these rites is the theological conviction that the natural events of human lives are about the encounter with the paschal mystery of Christ in the church. They are irreducibly ecclesial; that is, they all celebrate important events in the lives of individual Christians by relating them to the faith of the community. They are set within the context of baptism and eucharist—the clear preference of the rubrics is that marriage, burial, thanksgiving for a child, and commitment to Christian service will take place in the setting of the eucharist. Even The Reconciliation of a Penitent, although it clearly respects issues of personal confidentiality, is a ministry of the whole church that "is exercised through the care each Christian has for others, through the common prayer of Christians assembled for public worship, and through the priest-

hood of the Church and its ministers declaring absolution" (BCP 446).

A careful look through this section on pastoral
offices will reveal material that is perhaps less well-
known than other parts of the prayer book, but which
is important in understanding the liturgical spirituality this prayer book attempts to recover. I have heard
it said that in our society we tend to talk about living
in such and such a community and doing this or that
kind of work, and that, incidentally, we go to St.
Somebody's Church. We tend to talk about living *in*
the world and going *to* church. In the early church, on
the other hand, Christians talked about living *in* the
church, in the new society of believers, and going out
to the world.

Several examples illustrate how the 1979 prayer
book intends to aid the recovery of this earlier perspective. The 1549 and 1552 prayer books restricted
the solemnization of marriages to Sundays or holy
days, where it would take place after Morning Prayer
and the Litany and prior to Holy Communion.[7]
Marriage was to be a public celebration in the midst of
the regular worshiping community. By the time of the
1662 prayer book, this ideal had been abandoned; certainly in earlier American prayer books as well marriages had become for all intents and purposes
quasi-private affairs, in church but essentially for
invited guests. The 1979 prayer book, however, clearly assumes that the congregation's Sunday celebration of the eucharist will be the model for
weddings—in fact, there is nothing to prevent the
marriage of members of the congregation from taking
place at the principal Sunday eucharist. Likewise, the

rites for the visitation of the sick in earlier prayer books reflected a medieval understanding of sickness and death, in which the rites were used essentially to prepare the sick person for death. The 1979 prayer book assumes that the rites for the sick are primarily an opportunity for the sick person to be identified more closely with the dying and rising of Jesus Christ in his body, the church.[8]

Even the service for burial assumes that the fundamental identity of a baptized Christian is in the gathered community of believers, the body of Christ: provision is made for communal prayers at the time of death, the body is received liturgically in church where a vigil of prayer may be kept, and The Burial of the Dead (with a clear preference for a celebration of the eucharist) is to take place "when the congregation has opportunity to be present." The collect that concludes the prayers of the people commends to God's care the departed "who was reborn by water and the Spirit in Holy Baptism" and prays that this death may recall to us Christ's victory over death and be an occasion of renewal of the faith of the church in God's love. The paschal character of the life of Christians is declared in no uncertain terms in the anthem sung at the final commendation of the body: "All of us go down to the dust; yet even at the grave we make our song: Alleluia, alleluia, alleluia." At this moment, with the paschal candle burning nearby, there should be no doubt that the life of a Christian comes from participation in the dying and rising of Christ by baptism, eucharist, and the church's life of prayer and service to the world.

～ Other Prayer Book Material

Other significant and useful sections of the prayer book include Episcopal Services, or liturgies at which the bishop ordinarily presides; Prayers and Thanksgivings for various needs and occasions; An Outline of the Faith; Historical Documents of the Church; Tables for Finding Holy Days, which locate the dates of Easter and other major feasts; and The Calendar of the Church Year. Although these are used less frequently than the services of baptism, eucharist, the daily office, and the pastoral offices, they are valuable materials that establish the pattern of our common prayer.

The episcopal services mark important points in the church's life. The ordination rites form the bulk of this material, and though seldom used in most congregations, their inclusion in the prayer book is significant. In the rites of the church we say what our life together as a community of faith means. In the ordination rites we see liturgies that envision a rich complementarity of ministries, lay and ordained. Particularly in the examinations the rites describe the church's understanding of the ministries of bishop, priest, and deacon. Lay persons assume their own liturgical roles in the celebration (as intercessors, presenters, readers, bearers of bread and wine). Whether a person is to be ordained to the diaconate, priesthood, or episcopate, he or she is seen to be first and foremost a member of the assembly of the baptized, one of the *laos*, the holy people of God. This is shown ritually in the instruction that at the beginning of the service the ordinand is vested in the common baptismal garment—the alb (or its variant, the surplice)—without any other vesture indicating ecclesiastical or academic rank or order.

An Outline of the Faith, or Catechism, and the doctrinal formulations in the section of Historical Documents of the Church are important statements of the church's attempts to describe its encounter with God in Christ in the power of the Holy Spirit. They are not, however, substitutes for that encounter. Worship is primary theology: when two or three are gathered together, the presence of Christ is assured. In baptism new Christians are reborn in the image of Christ. The word of God is proclaimed and made present. In the eucharist bread and wine become the body and blood of Christ. We who are many become that one body for the life of the world. The dying and rising of Christ is made real in us. We are drawn into the life of the Holy Trinity.

Statements of doctrine are reflections on that primary experience. They attempt to give intellectual shape and language to the church's experience of encountering the Holy One. Because the church exists in human history, that language is necessarily historically conditioned. To read the Definition of the Union of the Divine and Human Natures in the Person of Christ of the Council of Chalcedon (BCP 864) is to read a statement that is fundamental to the Christian understanding of the significance of Christ Jesus, yet it is also a fifth-century document reflecting the historical and intellectual concerns of that time. Likewise, the Articles of Religion, while important descriptions of the classic Anglican understanding of Christian doctrine, nevertheless reflect the particular history of religious controversy out of which they were born. In much the same way, the Catechism is simply a good modern example of this secondary theology—a concise description of how the church makes sense of its experience of God.

The Episcopal Church is a pragmatic church. By this I do not mean that it is practical and straightforward in all its ways, but that it emphasizes the behaviors, the habits, the practices that make up Christian living. The Episcopal Church is a pragmatic church with a mystical edge. To be a member of the church you do the perfectly ordinary things the church does. You gather to offer praise and to lament, to pray for the needs of the world, to take part in the most human of actions—the telling of stories, the birthing of new children, the sharing of a common meal.

To do these ordinary things, however, is to invite and risk being grasped by the living God. *The Book of Common Prayer* is an outline for what the church does to become itself, to become what it is by grace, the body of Christ. Behind the pages of the prayer book are structures that go deep into the heart of Christian belief and practice. The prayer book is an invitation to a lifelong relationship with God: Father, Son, and Holy Spirit. It is an invitation to a relationship with God in the community of all those who are learning to die and rise with Christ. We accept that invitation by opening the pages of the prayer book—and in the next chapter we will do just that.

Chapter 7

Liturgy in Action

For some time now our congregation has been printing the order of the liturgy with the texts and music needed by members of the congregation in one service booklet. It is increasingly common in the Episcopal Church today to find these booklets, rather than a bulletin simply listing page numbers to the prayer book and hymnal: the booklets are easier for newcomers to use, since no one has to juggle several books during the service. After using these service booklets for over a year, a member of the congregation came to me after church one Sunday. "When are we going to go back to the prayer book again?" she asked. "I miss it." I honestly did not understand her question. "We *are* using the prayer book," I responded. What I meant, of course, was that the eucharist we celebrated every Sunday was made up of the acclamations, prayers, and actions presented and outlined on the pages marked The Holy Eucharist: Rite II of *The Book of Common Prayer.* We had simply arranged them, together with music from *The Hymnal 1982,* in one format for ease of use—to aid our common prayer. At least that was the intention.

What my parishioner thought, however, was that we were celebrating the eucharist according to some new and slightly alien rite. Because we were not physically holding those red prayer books, somehow we were not using *The Book of Common Prayer.* We printed in the booklets only those texts that members of the congregation would need to say together, so texts that the priest, deacon, or reader said were not printed. They had to be heard, rather than read along with as they were spoken. As I explained to my parishioner what we were doing in the liturgy she said, "Oh, of course I recognize it's the same thing now. I just never thought of it without the book in front of me before."

✎ Prayer: Private, Personal, Communal

There was a time when Anglicans had one prayer book with one order provided for each of the various services of the church. There were few if any options given about what to say when or which prayers or forms ought to make up a particular act of worship. One simply had to open the book and read the rite from beginning to end. That time is past. Today there are decisions worshiping congregations must make: Rite I or II? Which form of the Great Thanksgiving? The prayers of the people? Will we use a confession of sin? Will there be a creed? It is not surprising that more and more congregations are printing much of the service in booklet form each Sunday.

The 1979 edition of *The Book of Common Prayer* may look like the prayer books from earlier times, but it is actually a resource library for pastoral liturgy—liturgy that is responsive to a growing variety of pastoral needs and situations. We have moved with strong currents of scholarship and changing social contexts over the past fifty years from an understanding of liturgy as primarily something that is *said* to something that is *done*. As we noted earlier, liturgy is not simply words on a page; it has a shape. That shape is first and foremost the action of an assembly of Christians who gather to do something. It is indeed common prayer, the prayer of the community. But it is prayer embodied not just in words, but in gestures and movements, in touches and tastes and sounds and aromas, in signs and actions. The words we use are an articulation of the meaning of what we gather to do. We assemble together in worship as church to "speak the meaning of God for our world."[1]

Over the past fifty years a revolution has been underway in our understanding of what it means for Christians to pray, particularly among the liturgical churches. As a child I remember being taught that the first thing I was to do when I came into church was to kneel down quietly in place to say my prayers of preparation. There were disapproving stares if a newcomer or a child disturbed the pre-service calm. As a teenager in the Episcopal Church, I remember the vigorous objections of people in my congregation to the introduction of the sharing of the peace, which seemed like an intrusion into their private piety. As one member of a congregation I once served said, "The great thing about our church is that you can come here to pray and be left alone; the terrible thing about our church is that you can come here to pray and be left alone."

In part, I believe this private vision of prayer has depended on a certain cultural milieu. In the minds of many people the Episcopal Church in the United States has been associated with upper-middle class customs and norms of good behavior. It was not usually considered good form to discuss faith, prayer, and one's relationship with God in public. A church in which prayer was seen to be largely a private matter—even in the Sunday gathering of the congregation—was a church in line with the cultural norms of its members. Episcopalians have not been alone, of course, in this private approach to the life of prayer, but the image of politely hushed individuals kneeling in silence until they are told to open their prayer books to such and such a page persists as a popular notion of what worship looks like in an Episcopal Church.

The very title of the prayer book has offered a challenge to this image, however. In a sense, the development of the 1979 *Book of Common Prayer* was an attempt to take the challenge seriously. We gather for *common* prayer. In the last several decades, liturgical reformers within Anglicanism and among Christians in general have sought to reclaim a more vigorous understanding and practice of the communal dimension of Christian prayer. For Christians, in a real sense, there is no such thing as private prayer. In fact, the word "private" shares a root with "deprivation"—*privatio* in Latin is to deprive. This is not to deny the importance of times of personal prayer; but even personal prayer is fundamentally ecclesial in nature. When Christians pray, they do so with the church, not in isolation, even if they are alone: we pray always "with Angels and Archangels and with all the company of heaven" (BCP 362).

The notion of Christian prayer as an essentially private conversation between an individual and God has been nurtured not just among reticent middle-class North Americans, but by centuries of liturgical practice. In the book of Acts we see early Christianity portrayed as a radically communal faith: Christians held all things in common, and no one was in want (Acts 2:42–45). We know that churches of the first two or three centuries were relatively small and that their worship on the Lord's Day was originally in the context of a communal meal. As the church grew, especially after the reign of Constantine in the fourth century, sheer numbers led to a significantly less intimate pattern of worship.

As the middle ages progressed and the church took on more and more emblems of the old Roman Empire, the character and theology of worship changed dramatically too. The communal ethic we see portrayed in Acts gave way to a system of private confession and absolution. As we noted earlier, the intimate eucharistic meals of the early churches became the ritually elaborate masses of the high middle ages, at which no one but the priest received Holy Communion. The essentially organic nature of ministry among the first Christians—Paul's image of the one body of Christ with a variety of distinct but interdependent gifts (1 Corinthians 12:4–13)—was forgotten as the church developed into an elaborate and monarchical hierarchy of clergy, with the laity more or less reduced to saying private prayers while the priests celebrated the mass.[2]

The explosive upheavals of the Protestant Reformation and the technological breakthrough of the printing press combined to produce *The Book of Common Prayer.* That individual worshipers might each have a copy of the words of the rite they celebrated was no less significant a change in the sixteenth century than the disappearance of the communal meal as a setting for the eucharist was in the second. While the prayer book was a means of ensuring religious peace and uniformity in England, it also tended to atomize the church when Christians gathered for prayer. As a priest I have had the experience many times of offering the ritual greeting "The Lord be with you" to an assembly of worshipers only to be greeted by the response "And also with you" muffled by the books held in front of everyone's faces. Episcopalians have had a tendency to focus on set texts at the expense of an appreciation of the deep structures undergirding those texts: a greeting has become a piece of liturgical drill rather than a human interaction. Ironically, a prayer book intended for *common* prayer has led at times to the obscuring of the liturgy as common action. The reforms of the prayer book in the last twenty to thirty years have been motivated by the desire to foster genuinely communal prayer, prayer that is not just ecclesial in theory but in experience as well.

∼ At Home with Ritual

In a chapter devoted to *The Book of Common Prayer* as a resource for pastoral liturgy, it is tempting to focus on the texts and what they allow or do not allow in order to adapt them to particular situations. But I do not believe that liturgy has to do simply—or even primarily—to do with texts. Liturgy is not words on a page, it is ritual activity. There are many "how to" books and manuals that do a fine job of suggesting ways that the prayer book services—words and actions—can be put together. The resource section at the conclusion of this book lists some of them I would particularly recommend. What is often not addressed, however, is that liturgy is fundamentally a human activity of making and communicating meaning. *The Book of Common Prayer* is a resource for this work. But with the prayer book we also bring the stuff of our lives: stories, buildings, the arts, the physical material for sacraments. It is out of all these things that a given liturgical act is constructed. How clearly the prayer book can speak the meaning of God for us depends in no small measure on how we make use of these other human realities.

Liturgy is the public business of the assembled church. It is a public work that uses the raw material of ritual to accomplish its purpose, the praise of God and the incorporation of human beings into the divine life. Good liturgy demands good ritual. If liturgy often falls short of accomplishing in any obvious way its purposes, it may not be because of faulty theology or spirituality or translations of texts. It may have to do with our lack of facility in human ritual. When ritual is foreign to us, liturgy is left off by itself somewhere in "a domain we visit but are never at home in."[3] By ritual I do not mean the sometimes arcane ceremonial details that belong to a certain kind of ecclesiastical (and usually clerical) subculture: "How many spoonfuls of incense do we put on the coals?" I mean the strong, repeated, and repeatable actions in which human beings find layers of meaning, which in some sense create and communicate meaning. The ritual of Thanksgiving dinner comes to mind, or family birthdays. At these ritual meals certain foods are served in particular ways; even the order of seating at table over time communicates memories and associations that have to do with the identity of those who gather.

And yet many people live today in a state of ritual impoverishment. In the new suburban community in which I lived for a time, it was rare to find a family that *ever* shared a common meal together. "Grazing" on the run had effectively replaced the ritual of the dinner table, and even when a meal was shared it relied almost exclusively on prepackaged "convenience" foods. Likewise, it was not many generations ago that communities and households practiced rituals at the time of death that included preparing the body, "laying it out" in the home, receiving visitors, and attending to the burial itself. Today, that complex of rituals has been replaced by the relative anonymity and efficiency of hospitals and funeral homes. I am often greeted with polite incomprehension when I suggest to grieving relatives that *The Book of Common Prayer* envisions the practice of receiving the body of a Christian in church (and not the funeral home) for a vigil of prayer prior to burial. These and other rituals that have long been bearers of meaning and the possession of the whole community are disappearing or being given over to ritual professionals.

～ Sacramental Minimalism

This ritual impoverishment in daily life is not unrelated to the way the liturgical celebrations in many churches have been minimalized. The issue is particularly important when we consider the ritual of major sacramental celebrations, because sacraments effect by signifying. They are signs that communicate; they convey what they signify; they are actions that give new meaning to things.[4] All of this is simply another way of stating what generations of young Episcopalians learned to repeat by heart from the catechism:

> *Question:* What are the sacraments?
> *Answer:* The sacraments are outward and visible signs of inward and spiritual grace, given by Christ as sure and certain means by which we receive that grace. (BCP 857)

So the giving of grace is sure and certain; God is faithful. But sacramental signs are not just given *to* human beings, they are *for* human beings. We are the custodians, the stewards of those signs. And if it is true that sacraments effect what they signify—that they communicate grace precisely by being signs of that grace—then it matters very much how well they are able to signify. The quality and character of the sign is important. Matter matters.

There is no question in my mind that a child baptized by having three drops of water sprinkled on her forehead truly has been buried with Christ and raised "to the new life of grace" (BCP 308). But it is not very obvious that death and resurrection is what we mean by this action. It is difficult to believe that someone has died and been reborn when baptism is a mere sprinkling of water—no one ever drowned from being dribbled on. Likewise, the anointing and signing with the cross at baptism is meant to be a sign of the royal priesthood of Christ into which we welcome the newly baptized. How well is that signified when it is reduced to a perfunctory smudging of oil from a piece of cotton in a small oil stock? That the newly baptized person now shares in the priesthood of Christ is doubtless; that this meaning is clear is very doubtful.

The bread of the eucharist is another obvious example of the importance of the signs we use. In the parish I serve, a couple of weeks after we began using large loaves of bread at the eucharist rather than pre-formed communion hosts, a church school teacher overheard the following conversation between two eight-year-old boys: "I sure like it when they give us bread at communion." "Yeah, I don't know *what* we were getting before." The Roman Catholic liturgical scholar Aidan Kavanagh has remarked that he never had any trouble believing communion was the Body of Christ; he had trouble believing it was bread. It is undoubtedly true that communicants receive the "Body of Christ, the bread of heaven" when that bread is in the form of conveniently dry and tasteless wafers. But it is an entirely different experience when the bread has been broken from one large, fragrant loaf. Although its purpose is to do far more than merely fill the stomach, the eucharist is a banquet and it should clearly be experienced as one.

My point is simply that the quality of a liturgical experience has to do with the quality of its fundamental signs. Sacraments effect by signifying.

Sacraments make real; they do not make true.[5] We do not baptize people so that God will love them. We baptize them to make God's choice and acceptance of them real by means of this sacramental action. The bread and wine of the eucharist is not somehow "more" the Body of Christ after the Great Thanksgiving than it was before. Sacraments are not magic acts and we do not force Christ to be present in places Christ has not already chosen to be. The bread and the wine of the eucharist do not make the presence of Christ true, they make it real. And if the purpose of sacraments is to make these things real, then the quality of the signs themselves matters very much.

～ The Fundamentals of Liturgy

The first question, therefore, to be asked in planning or evaluating the significance of a liturgical act should be about the fundamentals that affect the quality of the sacramental sign. A list of these basic elements of liturgy would certainly include the bread and wine of the eucharist, the water and oil of baptism. And the list could go on to include other fundamentals that determine the effect a sacramental sign will have.

～ *Ministerial Order*

One of these fundamentals has to do with the ministers. The catechism makes it clear that the ministers of the church are lay persons, bishops, priests, and deacons. Is it equally clear that each of these ministries is exercising its distinctive role in the ordering of the church's worship as the prayer book directs? The assembly of the baptized is itself the primary minister of the liturgy—demonstrated among many other places in the dialogue at the beginning of the Great Thanksgiving, when the presiding priest or bishop asks the permission of the assembly to proceed in its name: "Let us give thanks to the Lord. It is right to give him thanks and praise." How obvious is it that this is so? Do the ordained ministers occupy one place in the room—perhaps elevated and even fenced off by rails—while the rest of the baptized sit passively in theater-style rows? What does the building *say?*

～ Liturgical Year

In the liturgical year, the church enacts the story of salvation. In the Christmas and Easter cycles we ritually encounter Christ's incarnation, earthly ministry, betrayal, passion, death, and resurrection. In the long seasons of Epiphany (after Christmas) and during the numbered Sundays of ordered time after Pentecost we consider the implications of these events for our life and mission. Is the congregation allowing the liturgical story to shape its life? How does the liturgical year inform educational and fellowship events? One parish I know has its biggest party of the year in the middle of Lent. Why not wait a few weeks so that Easter might be experienced to be more than what we do "in church"?

Is the liturgical year observed with strong ritual rhythm? Without being told, for instance, how would the congregation know that it was celebrating the eucharist in Lent? What does Advent feel like? What is the liturgical sense of continuing to kneel and say the general confession during the Fifty Days of Easter? Good ritual respects the power of repetition. What texts, melodies, sights, smells, physical arrangements are associated over time with the unfolding of the liturgical year?

∽ Font, Table, Scriptures

Is the altar table a powerful sign of the hospitality of God, beautiful and significant enough to stand on its own? Is it accessible to everyone so that it may be seen to be their banquet table? Or is it treated as a convenient surface to hold everything from the presider's glasses to the bishop's staff?

Is the baptismal font capable of communicating by its presence that here new Christians die with Christ and are reborn to new life? Or does its size and placement in the room say that baptism is something less important than that? Is there water in it that can be heard and seen and touched?

Where are the scriptures proclaimed? Is there one stand or lectern for the lessons read by lay persons and another, perhaps more exalted place, from which the deacon reads the gospel? Why?

∽ Music

Is music obviously a servant of the liturgical action or is it the other way around? Do hymns, for instance, intrude between the proclamation of the gospel and its explication in the sermon? Is it obvious that the choir and other leaders of music are ministers of the liturgy, that their first purpose is to lead the congregation in its praise of God? What is sung and why? Or why not? What is communicated, for instance, when five hymns are sung during a celebration of the eucharist—at the entrance procession, before the gospel, at the offertory, during communion, and before the dismissal—while the great acclamation in the eucharistic prayer, the *Sanctus*, is said?

～ Intention

Is the structure of the rite clear and direct? Do the various parts of the liturgy accomplish what they intend? For example, does the gathering rite actually gather the assembly? In most Episcopal churches the opening acclamation, a strong setting of the *Gloria* or some other song of praise, and then the collect of the day should be sufficient to gather the assembly into a body prepared to hear its scriptures. Throwing in all the possibilities—processional hymn, acclamation, collect for purity, *Kyrie*, *Gloria*, and collect of the day—is liturgical elaboration that may simply obscure the purpose of the gathering rite and eclipse the importance of what follows.

The rubrics direct that representatives of the congregation are to bring the peoples' offerings of bread, wine, money, and other gifts directly to the deacon or priest (BCP 361). Representative members are offering signs of their life and labor. Is the meaning of this essentially simple action encrusted with processional crosses, flags, and other additions? Do the bearers of the gifts in fact bring them directly to the altar to be received by the deacon or do they have to be presented through a hierarchy of acolytes?

These are just examples of the kinds of fundamental questions that have to be asked if the liturgy of the church is going to be allowed to speak as clearly as possible. In the parish I serve we half-jokingly refer to the rector's job description as "to keep the main thing the main thing." I believe paying attention to these fundamental elements of the liturgy goes a long way toward keeping the main thing the main thing in the church's worship. They are essential in the work of planning and celebrating good liturgy.

～ Making Liturgy

I will never forget a meeting once with the members of a church vestry whose rector had just left for a new church. I was their consultant as they planned for the leadership transition time and search process. We were talking about all the aspects of the parish's life that were now solely in their hands. A parish tradition had been to celebrate Evening Prayer on a particular feast day; that day was coming up and the senior warden—in something of a panic—asked me to plan the liturgy. "Why don't you all plan it?" I asked. "Us?" he said. "We wouldn't have the first idea how to put that together." His response would certainly be shared by many in the church today, and I think that is a tragedy. The prayer book is the common property of every member of the church and every worshiper should know how to use it to create a simple liturgical act of worship, or at least know where to begin. How do we use the tools? What would you do if you were that senior warden? How would you plan that liturgical celebration?

The first thing to do when planning a liturgy is to consider the overall structure and intention of the gathering for worship. What do you intend to do in this act of worship? It is easy to think that liturgy is simply a series of words and actions strung together like beads. "This happens, then that happens, then this." It is true that liturgies are composed of a sequence of actions. But in planning liturgical prayer it is important to think not just of the individual texts and ceremonial activities and how they might be put together—not just what kind of beads are going on the string next—but of what kind of necklace you want to make in the first place. What is the purpose of a particular liturgical gathering? The lighting and setting of the worship space, the choice of particular texts, the style and "feel" of the music that is chosen, decisions about preaching and readings—all of these elements of the liturgy are at the service of the greater whole, and each colors all the rest. Liturgy is not simply a set of mechanical decisions, it is an art form. It is an art at the service of nothing less than the presence of the risen Jesus Christ present among the redeemed people of God.

In this case, the congregation needed a service of evening prayer that would be flexible enough to incorporate the celebration of a feast day for a congregation not accustomed to praying together in the evening on a regular basis. An Order of Worship for the Evening would be a good choice for them, because the order is just that: an outline providing ceremonial directions, texts, and structural suggestions for celebrating an evening office. It may be used as a complete office in itself, as the introduction to daily Evening Prayer or to an evening celebration of the eucharist or some other service, or in the home as prayer before a meal or some other activity. It is particularly appropriate for use as evening prayer by a congregation that does not gather regularly for the daily office, since the psalms and readings for daily

Morning and Evening Prayer are read in course for the most part and might well make little sense to a congregation that has not followed it.

Once you have identified the overall purpose of the liturgy and chosen a particular form to use, before you walk through each element of the liturgy it is often helpful to turn first to the section in the prayer book called Concerning the Service. These guidelines offer suggestions for variations that may well be useful to you as you plan. One of the characteristics of this ancient form of the evening office, for example, is that it provides for the various orders of ministry to exercise their distinctive liturgical roles. In its section Concerning the Service (BCP 108) we are told that lay persons may of course lead the office, but that when the ordained officiate they should say the Prayer for Light, and that the bishop when present should bless the people at the conclusion of the office. A deacon could also lead the intercessions and give the dismissal. As you plan each element in this evening celebration you might therefore keep this diversity of ministries in mind when choosing leaders for various parts of the service.

⌁ Darkness and Light

The church is dark before the beginning of the service. This is an example of one of those fundamental issues of ritual too often overlooked. The power of this office is precisely in the action of light being kindled in the darkness—an image of the light of Christ. That power drains away when the act is reduced to a candle or two shining weakly in the glare of overhead lighting. We are also instructed that a musical prelude or processional is not appropriate before this service (BCP 142). The assembly gathers in the dark and silence.

In the Easter season the paschal candle would ordinarily already be burning in its place and the officiant would go to greet the people by its light. In other seasons, one or two candles could be carried before the officiant into the dark church. Other candles should be in place ready to be lighted after the prayer for light—at the altar, at other places in the worship space. Since our evening office is a special celebration, we might have small hand-held candles in the hands of worshipers.

As everyone stands the officiant greets the people with one of three acclamations provided. The optional short lesson of scripture that follows is best omitted when the order is used as a complete office with a scripture reading occurring later, as will be the case with our evening celebration. The short lesson is appropriate, however, when the light service is being used as an introduction to a meal or some other activity.

The officiant then leads the Prayer for Light. The rubric says that one of the prayers printed may be used "or some other suitable prayer" (BCP 110). Here we might also choose to pray the collect for the feast day we are celebrating. Prayers often assume great ritual power when beautifully sung. The purpose of this prayer is to bless God for the gift of light, the light of our flame on this occasion as a sign of the Light of the world, Jesus Christ. After the prayer, other candles and lamps in the worship space are lighted. During this action silence may be kept or an anthem may be sung.

The climax of this section of the liturgy comes now in the singing of the evening hymn, *Phos hilaron*, O Gracious Light. The prayer book suggests that incense may be burned during the evening hymn, a custom that may have originated ultimately in the daily offering of incense in the temple (see Exodus 30). Its most immediate predecessor would be the use of incense at the lamp lighting in Jewish homes on the sabbath and festivals, and symbolizes the rising of prayer to God, together with the prayers of the saints—imagery from the book of Revelation. Psalm 141 is traditionally associated with the evening office: "Let my prayer be set forth in your sight as incense, the lifting up of my hands as the evening sacrifice." The incense could be burned in a large bowl placed where the rising smoke is seen as well as smelled.

∾ Psalms

The next element in the evening office is a selection from the psalter. In addition to Psalm 141, the prayer book suggests thirteen other psalms appropriate for use in the evening (BCP 143). Whenever possible the psalms should be sung. The psalter is a hymnbook and there are endless musical resources to allow a congregation of any size and capability to sing them. Each psalm may be followed by silence and/or a collect. The prayer book does not provide specific collects for this purpose, but these may be drawn from elsewhere in the prayer book or from other sources. For example, *The Book of Alternative Services* of the Anglican Church of Canada prints the psalter with an appropriate prayer following each psalm.

～ Proclamation of Scripture

A reading from the Bible follows the psalm(s). Since our celebration is to take place on a major feast day, the reading might be taken from those appointed for the celebration of the eucharist. A silence might follow the reading, and a homily or a passage from Christian literature, such as writings from the patristic period relating to the feast day or occasion, or accounts of the lives of the saints.

The congregation then responds to the proclamation of scripture in song. This could take the form of the traditional evening canticle The Song of Mary, or "some other hymn of praise." *The Hymnal 1982* contains a wealth of chant and metrical settings of the canticles in the prayer book.

～ Intercessions

After the canticle comes intercessory prayer, possibly in the form of a litany. The Orthodox-style litany from daily Evening Prayer would be appropriate here (BCP 122), or a form of the prayers of the people as at the eucharist. Again, for many the prayers take on a greater ritual weight when they are sung rather than said. The intercessions are concluded and the prayers gathered into the words of the Lord's Prayer.

～ Conclusion

An Order of Worship for the Evening may end with a blessing and/or dismissal. The service might also conclude with the peace.

～ Pastoral Liturgy and the Mission of the Church

The mission of the church is to make disciples of all people, baptizing them in the name of the Triune God so that they might be restored to unity with God and one another in Christ (BCP 855). As the catechism suggests, this mission is accomplished in different and interdependent ways: as the church prays, worships, proclaims the gospel, and works for justice and peace. But it has been my experience that our worship in particular is one of the most powerful tools we possess for the work of evangelization. In the Anglican tradition worship and the mission of the church are inextricably linked.

It is not uncommon to find adult believers in the Episcopal Church who came into this church because of attendance at an act of worship, nor is it uncommon to find mature Christians in this church who can describe a significant deepening of their relationship with God in Christ as a result of worship. It is possible to hear the stories of children and adults in this church who were introduced to Jesus Christ as a living presence by their participation in the liturgy. I think of the four year old who had come to the altar with her father and mother since infancy to receive only a blessing and who one Sunday reached out both hands for the eucharistic bread and said, "I want Jesus too." I think of a young adult woman who after a year of inquiry asked for baptism—all because she had been so moved by the singing of a hymn in the church she wandered into one Sunday by chance. I think of the elderly parishioner living with

Alzheimer's disease who could still join in the Lord's Prayer when he could remember almost nothing else.

Michael Ramsey, the 100th Archbishop of Canterbury, in an address in 1963, spoke about the liturgy of the church as "divine gift" and "human response." He said that Anglican liturgy in all the forms it has taken throughout the world was particularly mindful of both the one sacrifice of Calvary and the heavenly priesthood of Christ as an ongoing reality in the lives of Christians. He said, "Today liturgical movements in many parts of Christendom put a renewed emphasis upon the participation of the faithful in liturgy and upon the down-to-earth aspect of the liturgy as the means of consecrating the common, everyday life of the people of God." In this way, said Archbishop Ramsey, the liturgy is foundational to the renewal of the mission of the church.[6] The renewal of liturgy represented in the 1979 *Book of Common Prayer* is linked deeply to the renewal of the church's mission to "restore all people to unity with God and each other in Christ" (BCP 855). But the book is merely a resource in this renewal. And as with any resource or tool, it will not use itself. It is up to faithful worshiping communities to use it fully and well.

From the beginning, the prayer book tradition has been about leading people into worship in language that they can understand. It has been about making the ancient pattern of the tradition of Christian worship a living reality. It has been about pastoral liturgy, liturgy that is responsive to the lived experience of the people of God. This is of such importance because common, everyday life (to use Michael Ramsey's words) is the raw material of the sacramental presence of Christ. Worship is such a powerful means of evangelism because in our worship Christ is truly present—and present by means of the assembled congregation itself. Pastoral liturgy is supremely aware of this mystery and honors it. The prayer book has changed and grown because the sacramental raw material of our lives has changed. The language of life has changed and continues to evolve.

Today, the question of language that is understandable is going far beyond questions of contemporary English versus Elizabethan poetry. Legitimate questions are being raised, for example, about the use of exclusively masculine images for God in our liturgical prayer. But there are equally important questions to be raised about the powerful language of architecture, suggesting as it does in many of our churches a separation between the baptized and their ordained servants, that God is only somehow "up there," and that the role of worshipers is to be passive observers of a sacred production.

Responding to these and many other modern questions has brought about a change in the prayer book tradition itself in two fundamental ways: it has grown more complex while it has become simpler. It has grown more complex in the range of options that are now available for individual congregations to craft their own liturgical life. It is really no longer even possible to speak of "the prayer book" as one invariable text. One has to ask, which prayer book, or supplement, or form? But if the prayer book tradition has grown more complex in terms of the range of texts available for use, it has also grown simpler in its understanding of the fundamental shape of the actions those texts serve to articulate. The prayer book cannot be reduced to a set of texts. *The Book of Common Prayer* has always been more than a book and it is more than a book today—it is a pattern for the Christian life, a way of being church.

Chapter 8

Looking Toward the Future

The prayer book as we have it today may be the last one of its kind. The General Convention of the Episcopal Church, meeting in Philadelphia in 1997, directed the Standing Liturgical Commission to prepare a plan "for liturgical revision and enrichment for the worship of the church, reflecting its multicultural, multiethnic, multilingual, and multigenerational character." The General Convention further directed that the revised texts, when authorized, should be made available "in a variety of forms, including multimedia and electronic options." Indeed, *The Book of Common Prayer*, *The Book of Occasional Services*, *Lesser Feasts and Fasts*, and *Enriching Our Worship* are already available to congregations in CD-ROM format. It is easy to imagine a time in the near future when electronic resources will be more important than printed books in preparing liturgical worship.

It may well be that one book in any form is insufficient to meet the needs of an increasingly diverse church in an increasingly complex world. For some Anglicans that is a threatening idea. We have lived for many years with a "myth of liturgical uniformity,"[1] the idea cherished by many worshipers that they could visit a parish anywhere in the Anglican world and know the service by heart. Today, in the same North American city on any given Sunday, it would not be unusual to find one Episcopal congregation worshiping in Spanish with traditional folk music, another celebrating the eucharist according to Rite I with medieval ceremonial and chant, and another gathering informally using supplemental inclusive language texts.

While it may no longer be the case that Episcopalians can expect to hear exactly the same *words* in any congregation they happen to visit, it is true that they can expect to encounter the same *actions*. We may use different words in different places, but we gather intending to do the same things: to wash new Christians in Holy Baptism and to celebrate the mystery of Christ's presence with us in the Holy Eucharist. And we do those things with a sense of identity that cannot be reduced simply to the use of uniform verbal formulas. We may not see another printed, bound version of *The Book of Common Prayer* authorized for use throughout the church as in the past. Instead, we may have a variety of printed or electronic resources. But even with these new forms Episcopalians will continue to worship according to the prayer book tradition.

❧ The Prayer Book and Culture

Thomas Cranmer's prayer book—in whatever version—is no longer the glue holding the identity of the Anglican Communion together. From the alternative service books in the Church of England and the Anglican Church of Canada to new prayer books in New Zealand, Australia, and South Africa, the current and planned revisions of *The Book of Common Prayer* throughout the Anglican Communion bear little obvious resemblance to the words and patterns of the sixteenth-century original. I remember my seminary professor of liturgical theology, Louis Weil, calling our own 1979 prayer book "the last Band-Aid on Cranmer." The 1979 prayer book may well be the last one to incorporate elements of Cranmer's work that have not been radically reshaped, such as the Rite I eucharist. These changes in the prayer book are for perfectly good reasons, as Leonel Mitchell has noted: "Language changes. Culture changes. Our worship is conditioned by both and must change in order to remain the same."[2]

Underlying the multiplication of versions of the prayer book are important questions having to do with inculturation. Someone in one congregation I know was showing slides of a recent trip to Africa to a church's adult forum group. One picture portrayed a group of Anglican African bishops standing in what looked like the heat of the midday sun. They were dressed in the traditional Anglican episcopal robes called rochets and chimeres. The rochet is a version of the alb or surplice, the chimere a sleeveless garment in black or red. In Victorian times the sleeves of the rochet were balloon-like with ruffles at the wrists—

the bishops in this photograph were dressed similarly. "It sure looks like it must have been hot," said someone in the room. "Yes," said the presenter, "I reckon it was hovering around 100 degrees that day." "Then why," asked someone else in the room, "are those bishops dressed in nineteenth-century English riding habits?"

Social norms, forms, and figures of speech, even mannerisms and customary ways of dressing, may not make sense when simply transferred from one cultural context to another. They often require translation or radical transformation. The realities to which they point and the values they embody may require entirely different structures that are indigenous to the new setting. This is no less true of the gospel of Jesus Christ and the worship of the church than it is of far more trivial matters.

But that translation is not simple. In a recent article, one author criticizes so-called multicultural liturgies that are essentially white Anglo celebrations with a fashionable smattering of elements from other cultural traditions.[3] Such celebrations, when they are planned, produced, and owned by a dominant cultural group, usually under the banner of "inclusivity," succeed only in reinforcing the message that this is "our" church and that "you" have graciously been invited to be a guest. Ultimately, liturgical inculturation means trusting that the patterns of Christian worship will find faithful new expression in the communities that come to own them.

The challenge of inculturation goes far deeper than simply translating prayer book texts into languages other than English. In one Hispanic congregation I know the Anglo rector knows just enough Spanish to preside at the eucharist—he preaches in English, however, and a member of the congregation translates. When I asked why the translator or the Spanish-speaking deacon did not preach instead, I was told that "the prayer book doesn't allow it."[4] Our prayer book tradition at times can become a kind of liturgical imperialism or fundamentalism that confuses style with substance. I think back to the story of two church communities in Nicaragua with which this book began. To the eyes of this North American visitor, one of those communities had taken the fundamental pattern of the eucharist and made it their own—even though that meant reshaping or disregarding the "rules" of the official liturgical rite. The other community appeared to be celebrating the eucharist with great attention to the rubrics, but in a cultural language foreign to the land.

The early history of the Episcopal Church in the United States is itself an illustration of a kind of inculturation, leading over time to substantial reshaping of the tradition. The hierarchical model of episcopal ministry as it was known in England, with all its political overtones, was clearly not workable in the new context. The ministry of bishops was preserved for this church by altering significantly the way in which that ministry was exercised. Episcopal ministry changed in order to remain the same. Likewise, while it may have seemed to some that *The Book of Common Prayer* required only minor adjustments in its language, as we have seen, the story of the American prayer book involved much deeper changes for the sake of the mission of the church in its new context. The prayer book changed in order to remain *The Book of Common Prayer.* When the General Convention of the Episcopal Church called for a plan to revise the prayer book, it did so with questions of inculturation in mind. How can local communities of Christians, in all their cultural diversity, come to own the prayer book liturgies? Will words and actions that are appropriate for a middle-class, suburban congregation have the same kind of power for other kinds of communities?

What is necessary in the task of liturgical incultur-ation is to distinguish clearly that which is essential to Christian faith from that which is not. The outward "dress" of the church's worship has changed dramat-ically—words, ceremonial, architectural setting—but the fundamental pattern has remained clear. Knowing this pattern fully and exploring its boundaries becomes the real work of liturgical inculturation.

∿ Ordered Freedom

The essential pattern of the prayer book tradition allows for a great deal of freedom. And as the prayer book grows in complexity in terms of the variety of forms and texts in use throughout the Anglican Communion, almost paradoxically the simplicity of its fundamental pattern becomes clearer. The essential shape of the liturgy of the church has emerged with increasing clarity over the last fifty years even as the variety of rites and styles and texts has grown. A seri-ous case can be made that the enterprise begun by Thomas Cranmer in restoring genuinely common prayer in the church has come to a significant stage of completion only in our own time. And this is true even as the task of prayer book revision has passed from being the concern solely of official experts more and more into the hands of local worshiping communities. The task, of course, is never over: no version of the prayer book, no liturgical form can claim that kind of finality. The prayer book tradition itself stands as a witness to the need for continual renewal.

Far from being a threat to a sense of Anglican identity, then, the growing complexity of the prayer book tradition can be viewed as a natural outcome of something fundamental to Anglicanism itself—its sense of ordered freedom. The Anglican tradition has demonstrated a remarkable capacity to embrace change as a means of remaining faithful to its mission in the world. And this capacity is a result of a deeply rooted characteristic of Anglican spirituality: its pragmatic sensibility and freedom to adapt—a freedom shaped by the liturgy of *The Book of Common Prayer* itself.

The word "freedom" has with a whole host of meanings and associations. For a great many people in western societies the word has come to mean primarily the freedom to choose from among more and more individualized options that suit *me*. I can choose this product or that one, this model computer or another one. In other words, like many other aspects of our consumer-oriented society, the word "freedom" has taken on profoundly individualistic, privatized connotations. I am free to do whatever suits me at the moment, whatever meets *my* needs. The multiplication of texts and rites might easily be seen to invite this kind of approach to liturgical celebration—a liturgical superstore where I can pick and choose to my heart's content.

But this is not the way the word is used in the Christian tradition. Already in the letters of Paul we see the working out of a certain tension between freedom and order. In Paul's first letter to the Corinthians he takes the church community to task for not realizing that their freedom in Christ has certain boundaries. "Of course you're free from laws prohibiting the eating of meat that was ritually offered to idols," says Paul. "But if your eating of that meat causes someone else in the community to stop growing in the faith, don't do it." Paul tells them later that their eucharist (at this point it was still in the context of a full meal) is a betrayal of itself when those who are wealthy provide lavish spreads for themselves while others go hungry (1 Corinthians 8, 11). Individual freedoms, says Paul, are to be freely constrained and ordered by the community's commitment to building up the one body of Christ so that we may become the people God has created us to be.

This sense of the ordered freedom of Christians finds its classic Anglican expression in the work of Richard Hooker. The early church viewed its structures, ministries, and liturgy as a means of living into the freedom of Christ. When Hooker wrote his massive defense of Anglicanism, *The Laws of Ecclesiastical Polity*, he restated the early church's conviction that ecclesiastical structures and doctrines exist for the sake of freedom in Christ. Human beings are made for joy and the contemplation of God, he declared, and the disciplines of the church exist for that purpose. Hooker believed that certain aspects of the church are basic and fundamental, while others can and do change over time. Things like the Bible, the sacraments, and basic practices of prayer are fundamental because they have to do with revealing and encountering the person of Christ. Other issues, like the shape of the church's ministry, are important but secondary issues.

Anglicans since Hooker have had a sense that freedom is not simply the chaos of individuals picking and choosing to do their own thing, but the freedom that tends toward the goal of communion, of growing into the stature of Christ, who freely chose the way of the cross as the way of real life. Anglican freedom has identifiable patterns, but patterns with room for enormous variety. The famous tripod of scripture, reason, and tradition is one such pattern. But so is *The Book of Common Prayer.* The purpose of the prayer book, its ordering principle if you will, is to provide a way of being church that will lead communities and individuals deeper into the freedom of Christ. Deeper into communion with God and so with one another. Deeper into the mystery of death and resurrection.

This is why Anglicans are not simply free to "do their own thing" liturgically. We live within the boundaries of a particular pattern. We have a great deal of freedom, particularly in the 1979 prayer book, with its options and flexibility, and even more freedom now with the provision of alternative liturgical texts. The pattern can be expressed in wonderfully diverse ways. But there are boundaries. There is a pattern to our worship life we are bound to explore for the sake of the kind of freedom Paul talks about, the freedom of communion.

Rowan Williams, the bishop of the Diocese of Monmouth in Wales, tells a story about the

Benedictine monk who was his spiritual director for many years. This monk belonged to a very strict order in which the daily office was observed with great formality. His friend told him that on more than one occasion he would be deep in the middle of a pastoral encounter when the bell would ring and he would simply get up to go off to chapel. The person to whom he had been talking would say, "You can't just leave now!" And the monk always had the same reply: "If I didn't go now and say my prayers, I'd be of no use to you at all." And Williams says that there was ample evidence in the ministry of this monk that he was right. The discipline of a certain way of praying—a pattern and order of liturgical prayer—had shaped him into the kind of person who was free and open enough to hear whatever people had to bring him. The discipline led to a great freedom, a freedom *for* others.

I know in my own life there was a time when I was very conscious of following all the religious rules I could get my hands on. When I was in college I remember leaving angrily in the middle of a celebration of the eucharist once because the priest was taking great liberties with the prayer book rubrics. Apart from revealing my own character flaws, when I think back on it now this incident illustrates for me my inability at that time to appreciate the goal of ordered prayer. I did not understand the underlying pattern of liturgical prayer. I was stuck in the particular version of that pattern that I judged to be correct. In the years since that time I have found myself becoming more and more open to "alternative" ways of structuring liturgical prayer—I have become freer—the more I have come to understand its fundamental nature.

Liturgy is not something that is right or wrong. The pattern of the liturgy exists to form the community of faith into the image and likeness of Jesus Christ—*that* is the criterion by which any liturgical action must be evaluated. I now recognize that some of what I judged to be liturgical aberrations at that liturgy I attended in college were very appropriate ways of worshiping with a community of students.

Today, the discipline of liturgical pattern is more important than ever. As new texts are written and ways of celebrating common prayer grow increasingly diverse, it is important for worshiping communities to know thoroughly the tradition of their prayer. Not for the sake of liturgical correctness, but for the sake of the gospel. To know the classic shape of a eucharistic prayer is not important because it is an interesting piece of historical detail. It is important because it expresses the relationship of the church to the living mystery of the Triune God. Should new texts be written to express that relationship in images that speak from contemporary experience? Of course. But those texts must be subject to the liturgical discipline of the community and the patterns of its ongoing life.

After a remarkable presentation on the Trinity at the 1995 Trinity Institute, theologian Elizabeth Johnson responded to questions from callers who had participated from satellite downlink locations. One caller asked her opinion about using alternatives to Father, Son, and Holy Spirit in the liturgy—Mother, Child, and Spirit, for example, or Maker, Redeemer, and Sanctifier. Her answer was immediate and clear. She said that communities that are deeply engaged in the underlying theological questions about trinitarian relationship might well experiment with expanded liturgical language as one way—but only one way—of recovering a deeper appreciation of the mystery of the Holy Trinity. Communities that are not so engaged, said Johnson, should "leave it alone." Experiments with liturgical language should not be undertaken lightly, she said. Liturgical discipline demands theological engagement.

Liturgical discipline also demands conversation and communion. Our General Convention has urged congregations to use the authorized supplemental texts to develop their own materials, but to do so in communion with the broader church: liturgical experimentation is encouraged but subject to the communal discipline central to the church's life. Some experiments will likely come to be seen as outside the boundaries of the Christian liturgical pattern. But communities that are in life-giving relationships with one another and churches that know the fundamental communal patterns of the Christian liturgy can and should be entrusted with the task of actively participating in the evolution of the tradition.

～ Liturgical Spirituality: Variety and the Steady Beat

In recent years the realm of science known as chaos or complexity theory has entered the popular imagination as a way of viewing the world. Everything from organizational management to theology has been affected by the insights from this somewhat obscure district of the physical sciences. In fact, one of the most accessible introductions to complexity theory I know about was written by a business consultant.[5] I believe there are insights from chaos and complexity theory with profound implications for how we view the church's liturgical tradition of ordered freedom.

Physicists now describe reality as a constantly changing web of relationships, which at first glance might seem to be a description simply of chaos, disorder, absolute unpredictability. This is not the case, however. When a system seems to be in disorder, change is unpredictable and we call that chaos. What has emerged from the serious study of chaotic systems, however, is the truth that if we look at a system long enough and with enough perspective, it will display a pattern. The computer has made possible stunning images of chaotic patterns. Called fractals, these images result from non-linear mathematical equations run through countless iterations and plotted as points in three-dimensional computer phase space. The equations are free to evolve in an absolutely random fashion, chaotically. But what emerges from the chaos as the system evolves is order and pattern, a kind of beautiful complexity. Amazingly, the shape of the overall pattern can be observed at magnification factors in the trillions. In other words, the apparent chaos is shot through with order.

Fractals are models of physical systems that occur everywhere—the evolution of a weather system, say, or the leaf of a tree. The visual image shows that these physical systems never repeat themselves exactly; they are in that sense unpredictable. But in the infinite variety of the repetitions they demonstrate remarkable patterns. The system is free to repeat itself with infinite variety, but that freedom is ordered. The most chaotic of systems never goes outside certain boundaries. No two snowflakes are the same, but we know a snowflake when we see one. The human face appears in infinite forms, but we know it as our own.

If you look at the computer-generated models of these physical systems you will notice that there is something almost like a center of gravity around which the pattern gathers. In the language of fractals, this point around which the chaotic order emerges is called a "strange attractor." As I learn more about this way of looking at reality, I find myself wondering if there is something like a "strange attractor" for Anglican liturgy, a center around which the growing complexity of our liturgical tradition forms an identifiable pattern. I believe there is a deep point of contact here with the mystery of the Holy Trinity—God as relationship—and with the mystery of the death and resurrection of Jesus Christ as the pattern for all reality.

I was once helping to lead a gathering of clergy from around the country in a week-long conference. In the liturgies we had prepared for the conference we planned to use music from the ecumenical monastic community of Taizé. This community has developed a distinctive style of chant that has become increasingly popular in recent years. A typical arrangement has the congregation singing a portion of a psalm or canticle in a refrain that repeats over and over again. A cantor or cantors might sing the verses of the psalm on top of the ostinato chant being sung repeatedly by everyone else. At this particular conference the director of Trinity Institute, Fred Burnham, was scheduled to make a presentation on chaos and complexity theory. After the opening liturgy, during which we had used one of these chants, he came up to me and said, "What you've got there is a musical fractal!" The musical phrase repeats itself, but because it is sung by a living, breathing, human assembly, it is never precisely the same.

And that is a picture of the church's liturgical life. Because they are prayed by living, breathing, human assemblies, the forms contained in *The Book of Common Prayer* are never precisely the same. These insights from the world of physics and mathematics point to the lived reality of the church's worship through its long history, and they point to a liturgical spirituality that is unanxious about the growing diversity and complexity of the future of worship. The doctrine of the Trinity speaks of God's very nature as dynamic relationship. Increasing complexity appears to be what God is up to in creation. Diversity, variety, and change are natural signs of health and vitality.

The poet and organizational consultant David Whyte uses a powerful image from medicine to make the same point. The surest sign of a heart about to die, he says, is an absolutely regular, dull, and unwavering heartbeat. If a heart in that state is disturbed it can very suddenly go into total shutdown or careen completely out of control. A healthy heart varies its rhythm and rate of blood flow with every movement of the body, but it displays a remarkable consistency over time. A healthy heart can encounter many disturbances and always settle back into a life-giving beat.[6] I would add that a healthy heart does not beat like this all on its own, but because it exists in a complex web of relationships with other organs and bodily systems—"The heart cannot say to the stomach, 'I have no need of you'!"

As worshiping communities experiment with liturgical forms, as new texts are produced by individuals and committees, as ritual elements from native cultures are taken into the worship of local Christian assemblies, a healthy liturgical spirituality will settle into a life-giving beat. I believe this means that congregations should craft the shape of their worship and then stick with it for a while. Let a liturgical rhythm emerge. I have heard it said that "Episcopalians don't like to be surprised." Behind this observation may lie an important principle. We ask the liturgy to bear an enormous weight of meaning. Good ritual that is capable of bearing such weight depends on a certain familiarity so that the forms, actions, and texts can become vehicles for the meaning they embody. If members of the assembly have to wonder what is going to happen *this* Sunday morning, it can lessen their ability to worship. If they have to worry about getting the words right, or how to follow the liturgical action, they may be less free to encounter the Mystery of Christ in those words and actions and, above all, in one another.

～ Exploring the Boundaries

The liturgical tradition of the Christian people is a living tradition. It has demonstrated through its history the ordered chaos that seems to be essential to all healthy living things. The idea that the liturgy (or any other aspect of the church's life) should be a monolithic, unchanging, and invariable reality is a relatively modern notion. What I hope to have shown in this book is a glimpse of the larger pattern of the Christian liturgical tradition by focusing on the particular area of that pattern represented by *The Book of Common Prayer.* The prayer book tradition has shown in its history, as it is showing today, one of the fundamental signs of being a healthy living thing: it is growing in complexity. And as that complexity has grown, the underlying shape and pattern of the tradition has become clearer. I would identify the major markers of that pattern to be the following:

Baptism: the fundamental centrality of baptism as initiation into the death and resurrection of Christ. The congregation is the primary minister of all liturgy. Baptism makes common prayer possible. All ministry—in the church and in the world— flows from the font.

Eucharist: the primacy of eucharistic assembly on the Lord's Day as a weekly renewal of baptismal identity. That identity is renewed in the breaking open of both the Word and the Bread. We gather to receive the Body of Christ so that we may be the body of Christ in the world. Our communion is assured and made real in the eucharist.

Daily Prayer: the offering of the day to God in morning and evening prayer and the sanctification of major life events and crises in the context of the gathered community of faith. Daily prayer is a clearer realization of the goal of common prayer— that it should touch and shape all of Christian life.

If these are the major features of the prayer book tradition, if they to some extent describe the boundaries of that pattern, then there is room for great variety in how they are realized in specific acts of liturgy. And the church has authorized a growing body of resources to allow congregations to craft their own pastorally appropriate liturgies. The question today occupying the attention of the church more and more is how far the boundaries extend. Two of the most obvious examples are the liturgical blessing of same-sex relationships and the use of non-gender specific language in scripture and prayer texts addressing God. It is beyond the scope of this book to explore these two topics in any depth, but I do want to suggest that it is possible to view these and other contemporary questions through the lens of the church's liturgical practice and pattern.

I was involved once in a search process with the vestry of a church looking for a new rector. One of the written questions to which I was asked to respond was this: "What should be the teaching of the Episcopal Church regarding human sexuality?" My response was perhaps a little glib, but I wrote, "I believe the answer to your question is in your question. Regarding human sexuality the Episcopal Church should *teach*. Teaching and learning demand the hard work of genuine conversation. Too much of what passes for teaching in this area is simply slogan slinging." I may have been flippant, but I meant what I said. I suspected that behind this particular question was an answer about which this search committee had already made up its mind.

Too often questions about the liturgy that push the boundaries are asked at this level. "Is this or that liturgical activity right or wrong? Is it permissible or not?"

The problem with yes or no answers is that no one learns anything. Surely Christian community is more demanding than that for those who want to practice it. It must be admitted frankly that certain practices have not been part of the liturgical tradition of the Christian people and others have been tried and rejected. But it must also be admitted that elements of the tradition we take for granted also were not always part of that tradition, and that things once regarded as definitive are no longer. The prohibition of the remarriage of divorced persons is an example, or the Bible's apparent endorsement of slavery. These things were once sources of enormous controversy in the church. They were resolved only through the hard work of the Christian community examining and reinterpreting its own tradition.

One of the identifying marks of the Anglican way is its willingness to engage the realities of contemporary experience. We have not been content simply to quote either scripture or tradition, but to interpret them in a reasoned and reasonable way in the service of the mission of the church. If it is to be faithful and vital, this work of interpretation requires an ongoing engagement with scripture and tradition. There are, for example, feminine images for God from within the tradition itself, images that have been largely excluded from public prayer; the tradition of Holy Wisdom personified in female images from the Apocrypha is an important example. The prayer texts from *Enriching Our Worship* make use of these images in the attempt to make our language about God in worship truer to the God in whom we believe. Similarly, we are beginning to ask if there are aspects of the tradition regarding the Christian household that need to be reinterpreted in light of the contemporary experience of gay and lesbian Christians. Does the tradition itself call for its own reinterpretation in order to be truer to the God in whom we believe?[7]

These are only two issues among many others that loom large in conversations regarding the need for prayer book revision. My own hopes for revision center around the complex of liturgical actions having to do with Christian initiation. I hope that the rites for the catechumenate now found in *The Book of Occasional Services* will be included in the next formal revision of the prayer book, together with the rites for the preparation of persons for the reaffirmation of baptismal vows. I would hope that by being included in the prayer book as an integral part of the baptismal liturgy the serious preparation of adults for baptism would be recovered and seen to be the central task of the church. I believe the practice of confirmation also needs attention, including dropping its historically confused title in favor of calling it what it is: the reaffirmation of baptismal vows. There are important experiments in many places with celebrating rites of passage associated with adolescence; these too might find a place in the next revision. Other voices are calling for a rethinking of the church's ordination rites in the light of a renewed appreciation of baptism as the fundamental sacrament of ministry. Still others want to see greater flexibility in forms for the daily office— daily prayer that can be genuinely popular. We have already mentioned issues of inculturation. As the realities of the world in which we live change there will be others.

∿ Common Prayer and Paschal Life

While planning for a funeral liturgy I am sometimes asked about the appropriateness of a eulogy delivered by a family member or friend. I am not enthusiastic about eulogies. My experience of them has been that they attempt to do so much they accomplish very little—except to prove emotionally painful to the eulogist. There is certainly a place for personal remembrances and loving recollections about the dead person's life, but the liturgy is not that place. Talking to a family whose loved one has just died is not the time to take stands on liturgical correctness, however, and I have presided at a good many funerals where there was in fact a eulogy.

But my own mother's funeral in 1997 reminded me of why I take the stance I do. She died after a fast and devastating battle with cancer at the age of 62. And at her funeral I have never been so grateful for what I can only describe as the business-like character of the rites of the church. At the center of those rites is not an emotionally wrenching talk about the best qualities of the one we loved. At the center of the church's rites is the proclamation of the mighty act of God in raising Jesus Christ from death and the "reasonable and holy hope" we share of being raised with Christ. When Christians gather to bury one of their baptized brothers or sisters, they do not retreat into sentimentality. They do not cover up the horrible reality of death. They look death in the eye and sing, "Alleluia." Even at the grave.

At my mother's funeral I remember looking at the coffin as it stood there in the choir of the church, covered in a white pall. And as I looked I noticed some discoloration at the bottom of the pall. At first I thought this was odd, since my mother's parish church is fastidious about such things. But then it dawned on me: I was looking at a water stain, the result of countless sprinklings of countless coffins with baptismal water. In funeral liturgies at St. John's Church, as the prayer book's final anthem is sung, the coffin containing the body of a baptized Christian is aspersed one last time with the water that is the sign of our identity in Christ. The pall is a ritual reminder of the baptismal garment and this one bore the stain of many sisters and brothers who had gone before, members of the dying and rising body of Christ. Even at the grave we make our song: Alleluia.

Common prayer is a way of life. It is a way of living into the reality of the paschal mystery of Christ. It is a way of living more and more *from* that reality, dying to self and living for others in Christ to the glory of God and in the power of the Holy Spirit. *The Book of Common Prayer* is a pattern for that common prayer and that common life. It is a pattern to be explored and lived. Thanks be to God.

Endnotes

∿ Chapter 1: What is Common Prayer?

1. Stephen Sykes, *Unashamed Anglicanism* (Nashville: Abingdon Press, 1995), xviii.

2. Theodor Klauser, *A Short History of the Western Liturgy*, 2nd ed. (New York: Oxford University Press, 1979), 58-59.

3. Gordon Lathrop, *Holy Things* (Minneapolis: Fortress Press, 1993), 5.

∿ Chapter 2: The Pattern of Prayer

1. Marion J. Hatchett, *Commentary on the American Prayer Book* (San Francisco: HarperCollins, 1995), 177.

2. Jaroslav Pelikan, *The Emergence of the Catholic Tradition*, vol. 1 of *The Christian Tradition: A History of the Development of Doctrine* (Chicago: University of Chicago Press, 1971), 9.

3. Lathrop, *Holy Things*, 19-20.

4. For a description of the parallels between Jewish ritual meals and early Christian eucharistic practice see Willy Rordorf, "The *Didache*," in *The Eucharist of the Early Christians*, trans. Matthew J. O'Connell (New York: Pueblo Publishing Company, 1978).

5. Here I rely on the analysis of R. T. Beckwith, "The Jewish Background to Christian Worship" in Cheslyn Jones, Geoffrey Wainwright, and Edward Yarnold, eds., *The Study of Liturgy* (New York: Oxford University Press, 1978).

6. *Ibid.*, 42

7. For an extensive description of the evidence for Jewish daily prayer at that time see Paul F. Bradshaw, *Daily Prayer in the Early Church* (New York: Oxford University Press, 1982).

8. Justin Martyr, *Apology*, in *Eucharist of the Early Christians*, 73.

9. Hippolytus, *Apostolic Tradition*, in R. C. D. Jasper and G. J. Cuming, eds., *Prayers of the Eucharist: Early and Reformed*, 2nd ed. (New York: Oxford University Press, 1980), 22.

10. *The Apology of Justin Martyr*, in Ray C. Petry, ed., *A History of Christianity: Readings in the History of the Church*, vol. 1 (Grand Rapids: Baker Book House, 1981), 21.

11. Richard Norris, "The Loss of Baptismal Discipline," in Michael W. Merriman, ed., *The Baptismal Mystery and the Catechumenate* (New York: The Church Hymnal Corporation, 1990), 29.

12. For illustrated examples of ancient and contemporary baptistries see Regina Kuehn, *A Place for Baptism* (Chicago: Liturgy Training Publications, 1992).

13. Hymn 302/303 in *The Hymnal 1982*, trans. F. Bland Tucker from the *Didache*.

14. The Greek word, *anamnesis*, carries stronger and richer connotations than the English "remember." *Anamnesis* has to do with making the past an ongoing and present reality.

15. See Josef A. Jungmann, s. j., *The Early Liturgy* (Notre Dame: University of Notre Dame Press, 1959), 64ff.

16. Early in the fourth century Eusebius of Caesarea wrote that the times of prayer were "observed by everyone in

every place." For this citation and the development of the early office I rely on William Storey, "The Liturgy of the Hours: Cathedral versus Monastery," in John Gallen, S. J., ed., *Christians at Prayer* (Notre Dame: University of Notre Dame Press, 1977).

∿ Chapter 3: The Prayer Book is Born

1. See Louis Bouyer, *Liturgy and Architecture* (Notre Dame: University of Notre Dame Press, 1967).

2. Norris, "The Loss of Baptismal Discipline," in Merriman, ed., *Baptismal Mystery*, 34.

3. A succinct description of the state of the liturgy at the end of the middle ages is found in the first chapter of G. J. Cuming, *A History of Anglican Liturgy* (London: Macmillan and Co., 1969).

∿ Chapter 4: The American Prayer Book

1. Quoted in William Sydnor, *The Prayer Book Through the Ages* (Harrisburg: Morehouse Publishing, 1997), 58.

2. Cuming, *History of Anglican Liturgy*, 186.

3. Charles Price and Louis Weil, *Liturgy for Living* (New York: The Seabury Press, 1979), 90. From 1552 onward the English prayer book placed the receiving of Holy Communion directly after the words of institution, and *before* any prayers referring to offering. This was an attempt to counteract the medieval emphasis on the eucharist as a repetition of Christ's sacrifice.

4. Sydnor, *Prayer Book Through the Ages*, 59.

5. For a detailed description of these elements and an assessment of Seabury's role in shaping the Prayer of Consecration, see Marion Hatchett, *Commentary on the American Prayer Book*, 359f.

6. For a succinct treatment of the impact of the Oxford Movement on Anglican worship see Louis Weil, *Sacraments and Liturgy: The Outward Signs* (Oxford: Basil Blackwell, 1983).

7. Sydnor, *Prayer Book Through the Ages*, 80.

8. Michael Moriarity, *The Liturgical Revolution* (New York: The Church Hymnal Corporation, 1996), 20.

9. Sydnor, *Prayer Book Through the Ages*, 105f.

10. Moriarity, *The Liturgical Revolution*.

11. Quoted in John Fenwick and Bryan Spinks, *Worship in Transition: The Liturgical Movement in the Twentieth Century* (New York: Continuum Publishing, 1995), 44.

12. For a concise history of Associated Parishes see Michael Moriarity's *The Liturgical Revolution*.

13. F. D. Maurice, "The Prayer Book, Considered Especially in Reference to the Romish System," in *Nineteen Sermons Preached in the Chapel of Lincoln's Inn* (London: John W. Parker, West Strand, 1849), 6.

14. Various versions of Anglican missals had appeared in the late nineteenth and early twentieth centuries. They were essentially attempts to incorporate as much as possible of current Roman Catholic practice into the basic shape of the prayer book service.

15. James E. Griffiss, *The Anglican Vision* (Cambridge, Mass.: Cowley Publications, 1997), 93.

~ Chapter 5: A Baptismal Church

1. Words by Friedrich von Spee; hymn 173 in *The Hymnal 1982* (New York: The Church Hymnal Corporation, 1985).

2. Hatchett, *Commentary on the American Prayer Book*, 251.

3. The idea that adult candidates are normative should not be taken to mean that there is something defective or inferior about infant candidates for baptism. It simply to say that

infants and young children are presented for baptism on the basis of the faith of the adult community of believers. See Ruth Meyers, *Continuing the Reformation* (New York: Church Publishing Inc., 1997), 197f.

4. For a thorough treatment of this history by a Roman Catholic scholar that includes a chapter on confirmation in the prayer book, see Gerard Austin, *Anointing with the Spirit, The Rite of Confirmation: The Use of Oil and Chrism* (New York: Pueblo Publishing Company, 1985), 65–81.

5. For a succinct description of the history of confirmation see Price and Weil, *Liturgy for Living*, 115ff.

6: The Boston Statement of the 1985 International Anglican Liturgical Consultation, quoted by William R. Crockett in "Theological Foundations for the Practice of Christian Initiation in the Anglican Communion," *Growing in Newness of Life: Christian Initiation in Anglicanism Today*, ed. David R. Holeton (Toronto: Anglican Book Centre, 1993), 49.

～ Chapter 6: The Eucharist and Daily Office

1. The Anglican monk Gregory Dix is perhaps the most notable promoter of understanding the eucharist in these terms through his enormously influential book, *The Shape of the Liturgy* (London, A & C Black, Ltd., 1982).

2. For more on the significance of the collect see Louis Weil, *Gathered to Pray: Understanding Liturgical Prayer* (Cambridge, Mass.: Cowley Publications, 1986).

3. For a thorough guide to creating intercessions see Ormonde Plater, *Intercession: A Theological and Practical Guide* (Cambridge, Mass.: Cowley Publications, 1995).

4. Hatchett, *Commentary on the American Prayer Book*, 383.

5. George Wayne Smith, *Admirable Simplicity: Principles for Worship Planning in the Anglican Tradition* (New York: The Church Hymnal Corporation, 1996), 64.

6. Kathleen Norris, *The Cloister Walk* (New York: Riverhead Books, 1996), 100.

7. Smith, *Admirable Simplicity*, 125.

8. See Leonel L. Mitchell, *Praying Shapes Believing: A Theological Commentary on The Book of Common Prayer* (Harrisburg: Morehouse Publishing, 1996), 207ff.

~ Chapter 7: Liturgy in Action

1. Lathrop, *Holy Things*, 5.

2. For a detailed treatment of this change in the concept of ordained ministry, see James Barnett's *The Diaconate: A Full and Equal Order*, rev. ed. (Valley Forge, Penn.: Trinity Press International, 1995).

3. Gabe Huck, *Liturgy with Style and Grace*, rev. ed. (Chicago: Liturgy Training Publications, 1984), iv.

4. Byron D. Stuhlman, *Prayer Book Rubrics Expanded* (New York: The Church Hymnal Corporation, 1987), 33f.

5. See Bernard Cooke, *Sacraments and Sacramentality* (Mystic, Conn.: Twenty-Third Publications, 1983), 57.

6. *To Believe is to Pray: Readings from Michael Ramsey*, James E. Griffiss, ed. (Cambridge, Mass.: Cowley Publications, 1996), 185f.

~ Chapter 8: Looking Toward the Future

1. Clay Morris, "Prayer Book Revision or Liturgical Renewal?" in *A Prayer Book for the 21st Century*, Liturgical Studies Three (New York: The Church Hymnal Corporation, 1996), 250.

2. Leonel Mitchell, in the introduction to *A Prayer Book for the 21st Century*, ix.

3. Juan Oliver, "Just Praise: Prayer Book Revision and Hispanic/Latino Anglicanism," in *A Prayer Book for the 21st Century*, 265ff.

4. While there are good reasons to expect that the presider at a eucharist will ordinarily also be the preacher, the prayer book does not, in fact, require this or forbid anyone else to preach.

5. Margaret J. Wheatley, *Leadership and the New Science: Learning about Organization from an Orderly Universe* (San Francisco: Berrett-Koehler Publishers, Inc., 1994).

6. David Whyte, *The Heart Aroused: Poetry and the Preservation of the Soul in Corporate America* (New York: Doubleday Dell Publishing Group, Inc., 1996), 225.

7. For an example of this kind of careful engagement with the biblical tradition in particular, see Thomas Breidenthal, *Christian Households: The Sanctification of Nearness* (Cambridge, Mass.: Cowley Publications, 1998).

Resources

A teacher of mine used to tell students, "I don't care what you read—just read *something*." The range of scholarly and popular resources for the liturgy is vast and there are lots of places to dive in. As a way to begin, I offer here a selection of materials that I have found particularly helpful as a student of Christian worship and a user of *The Book of Common Prayer*.

∾ Liturgical Resources

One book has never contained all the resources a congregation would ever need for worship: even when Anglicans had a prayer book with very few options, unofficial rearrangements of texts were used, supplemental prayers were taken from a variety of sources, and music was supplied by hymnals and other collections of song. The church as always needed to adapt its official rites to the particular circumstances of the people who celebrate those rites. Today, the use of supplemental material is greater than ever and shows no signs of decreasing.

The Episcopal Church has now in fact authorized a large body of supplementary material that may be used to deepen the prayer of the church. Most congregations will make at least some use of the following resources:

The Hymnal 1982. In addition to the familiar material in the pew edition of this hymnal, the accompaniment edition contains settings of canticles and other liturgical texts. There are complete settings of the noonday office and Compline, anthems for the liturgies of holy week and burial, and both plainsong and Anglican chants for the psalter.

Lesser Feasts and Fasts. This book contains collects and readings for weekday commemorations of saints and other occasions, including the weekdays of Advent, Christmas, Lent, and Easter.

The Book of Occasional Services. This volume includes services for the church year, such as Advent Lessons and Carols, and resources for pastoral issues, such as A Public Service of Healing. Perhaps most important, in this book are the rites of the Episcopal Church for the catechumenate—the preparation of adults for baptism—and the parallel rites for the preparation of parents and godparents for the baptism of a child, and the rites for preparing baptized adults for the renewal of baptismal vows.

The Altar Book, the *Book of Gospels*, and *Eucharistic Readings.* These ritual books contain texts conveniently arranged for liturgical use in volumes of appropriate size and importance. *The Altar Book* contains what is needed for the presider at the eucharist—prayer book texts with musical notation. *Eucharistic Readings* contains readings for the eucharist from the three-year lectionary, while the *Book of Gospels* contains only the gospel readings.

Besides these books, many congregations will make use of additional liturgical resources in the following areas:

Music: Many settings are available of psalms designed for use at the eucharist. *The Plainsong Psalter* and *The Anglican Chant Psalter* are two important resources, but they require some musical sophistication to be used well. The selection of simplified Anglican chants in the accompaniment edition of *The Hymnal 1982* can be used by virtually any group with very little practice. Church Publishing also produces the other "official" hymnals and collections of song of the Episcopal Church: *Lift Every Voice and Sing II: An African American Hymnal*; *El Hymnario*; *Songs for Celebration*; and *Wonder, Love, and Praise: A Supplement to The Hymnal 1982.*

Expansive Language: Enriching Our Worship is the title of the volume containing supplementary liturgical texts authorized by the General Convention. These texts are sensitive to issues of inclusive language and include alternative versions of existing prayer book material as well as canticles drawn from post-biblical sources and newly composed eucharistic prayers. These texts are authorized for the use of congregations subject to the direction of the bishop.

～ Other Anglican Prayer Books

Other churches of the Anglican Communion are also producing a wealth of liturgical materials. *The Alternative Service Book* of the Anglican Church of Canada is particularly useful for users of the 1979 *Book of Common Prayer* because of their similarity in style and content.

In recent years in the United States, perhaps the most popular prayer book from elsewhere in the Anglican Communion has been *A New Zealand Prayer Book*. Its version of the daily offices in particular have been used with increasing frequency in Episcopal Church gatherings. The New Zealand book represents a significant departure from the Cranmerian tradition. It contains liturgical material making use of bold images and forms from cultures native to New Zealand, as well as reflecting broader contemporary issues of expansive language, environmental concerns, and cultural diversity.

～ Commentaries and History of Christian Worship

For a thorough history of the prayer book and detailed notes on each of its sections, the definitive guide is Marion J. Hatchett's *Commentary on the American Prayer Book* (San Francisco: HarperCollins, 1995). A less detailed and more reflective commentary based on Leonel L. Mitchell's observation that Episcopalians are, above all, liturgical theologians, is Mitchell's *Praying Shapes Believing* (Harrisburg: Morehouse Publishing, 1996). Both of these volumes are useful in answering questions about the source or intent of particular sections of the prayer book.

William Sydnor's *The Prayer Book Through the Ages* (Harrisburg: Morehouse Publishing, 1997) is a very readable short history of *The Book of Common Prayer.* It explores in greater detail the historical material presented in this book. The story of our current prayer book is told from the perspective of the impact of the modern Liturgical Movement on the Episcopal Church in *The Liturgical Revolution* by Michael Moriarity (New York: Church Hymnal, 1996).

Standard works on the early history of Christian worship include Theodor Klauser's *A Short History of the Western Liturgy* (New York: Oxford University Press, 1979) and Josef A. Jungmann's *The Early Liturgy* (Notre Dame: University of Notre Dame Press, 1959). For essays with an ecumenical perspective on the history of the liturgy by major categories (the history of Christian initiation, the eucharist, the daily office, and so forth) from earliest times through the Reformation, see Cheslyn Jones, Geoffrey Wainwright, and Edward Yarnold, eds., *The Study of Liturgy* (New York: Oxford University Press, 1978). A significant new work by a Lutheran with particular sensitivity to the ecumenical consensus regarding major themes of liturgical history is *Christian Liturgy: Catholic and Evangelical* by Frank C. Senn (Minneapolis: Fortress Press, 1997).

Several volumes from Church Publishing offer excellent commentary and theological reflection specifically on the rites of the Episcopal Church. On baptism see Daniel B. Stevick's *Baptismal Moments; Baptismal Meanings* (1987) and a very important collection of essays on formation for baptism and ministry, *The Baptismal Mystery and the Catechumenate*

(1990); on the development of the eucharist, Byron Stuhlman's *Eucharistic Celebration 1789–1979* (1995); on the underlying rationale for daily prayer, Stevick's *Redeeming the Time* (1992) is a thought-provoking work, as is his commentary on the pastoral offices in *Occasions of Grace* (1996). One of the most helpful and succinct treatments I know of the rationale behind the practice of confirmation in *The Book of Common Prayer* is chapter three of Gerard Austin's *The Rite of Confirmation: Anointing with the Spirit* (New York: Pueblo Publishing, 1985). For an overview on the state of Christian initiation in general in the Anglican Communion today see the collection of essays *Growing in Newness of Life*, edited by David R. Holeton (Toronto: The Anglican Book Centre, 1993).

～ Liturgical and Sacramental Theology

To my mind one of the most exciting books to appear in recent years dealing with the meaning of liturgical worship is Gordon W. Lathrop's *Holy Things* (Minneapolis: Fortress Press, 1993). He uncovers the essential patterns of Christian worship and the challenge of making them our own. In a similar vein, Aidan Kavanagh's *On Liturgical Theology* (New York: Pueblo Publishing Company, 1981) leads the reader to fundamental questions about what it means to engage in the sort of activity we describe as liturgy.

At first glance William Seth Adams's book *Shaped by Images* (New York: Church Hymnal, 1995) seems to be written primarily for ordained persons—its subtitle is *One Who Presides*. It is, however, a rich introduction to the central themes of liturgical theology as they are experienced by worshiping communities. A similar kind of book, written in the wake of the Roman Catholic reforms of Vatican II, is Robert W. Hovda's *Strong, Loving and Wise* (Collegeville, Minn.: The Liturgical Press, 1983). Both books speak passionately and poetically about churches transformed by taking seriously their own reforms of liturgical worship.

On sacramental theology I would recommend two books in particular. A very readable and systematically organized introduction to sacramental theology is John Macquarrie's *A Guide to the Sacraments* (New York: Continuum Publishing Company, 1998). Macquarrie presents a traditional understanding of the sacraments from an Anglican perspective. For a somewhat freer reflection on the meaning of the sacraments, one that stays very close to the ordinary experience of what we call grace, see Bernard Cooke's *Sacraments and Sacramentality* (Mystic, Conn.: Twenty-Third Publications, 1983).

~ Ceremonial Guides

There are many "how to" books available as resources for putting together the services contained in *The Book of Common Prayer*. Many people think of these books as written primarily for the clergy or worship committees, and indeed they are most useful for those who are charged with planning and leading worship. But every active participant in prayer book worship could benefit from knowing more about the rites and ceremonies they celebrate. A good general introduction to the task of preparing liturgical celebrations is Daniel B. Stevick's *The Crafting of Liturgy* (New York: Church Hymnal, 1990).

Three volumes from Cowley Publications form a complete ceremonial guide to the services of *The Book of Common Prayer:* Howard E. Galley's *The Ceremonies of the Eucharist* (1989), and Leonel L. Mitchell's *Lent, Holy, Easter, and the Great Fifty Days* (1996), and *Pastoral and Occasional Liturgies* (1998). Another single-volume ceremonial guide is Byron Stuhlman's *Prayer Book Rubrics Expanded* (New York: Church Publishing, 1987). All these works offer specific helpful suggestions for realizing the intentions of the rubrics appropriately in various settings. Written from a Roman Catholic perspective but with obvious applications to the rites of the prayer book is Gabe Huck's *The Three Days: Parish Prayer in the Paschal Triduum* (Chicago: Liturgy Training Publications, 1995). This book offers an almost rhapsodic reflection on the liturgies of Maundy Thursday, Good Friday, and the Easter Vigil, together with practical suggestions for their celebration as the center of parish life.

Certain liturgical actions or ministries in the current prayer book still seem to generate debate, inquiry, or uncertainty in the church. Among these I would point to the role of the diaconate, the place, preparation for, and manner of baptism, and the crafting of the prayers of the people. On the liturgical role of deacons see: *Deacons in the Liturgy* by Ormonde Plater (Harrisburg: Morehouse Publishing, 1992) and *The Diaconate: A Full and Equal Order* by James Monroe Barnett (Valley Forge, Penn.: Trinity Press International, 1995). Barnett's book is an exhaustive look at the history and theology of the diaconate; its concluding chapters are directed at the liturgical role of deacons.

On questions of baptismal practice see *The Baptizing Community* by A. Theodore Eastman (Minneapolis: The Seabury Press, 1982—out of print but well worth finding) and a fine commentary on the revised service of baptism in the Anglican Church of Canada, *Into the Household of God* by John W. B. Hill (Toronto: Anglican Book Centre, 1994). A very helpful theological reflection on the importance of intercessions in the eucharist and a practical guide to their performance (complete with music) is Ormonde Plater's *Intercession: A Theological and Practical Guide* (Cambridge, Mass.: Cowley Publications, 1996).

The books mentioned above are quite specific in their suggestions and directions for putting together a liturgy. There are other books that address questions of liturgical style more broadly. An entertaining treatment of the fundamentals of liturgical celebration is Aidan Kavanagh's *Elements of Rite* (New York: Pueblo Publishing Co., 1982). Kavanagh writes as a Roman Catholic, but his observations are equally applicable to prayer book worship. Taking into account both history and current practice, George Wayne Smith raises issues about an appropriate overall style for the services of *The Book of Common Prayer* in his *Admirable Simplicity* (New York: Church Hymnal, 1996).

~ The Architectural Setting for Worship

The closest thing the Episcopal Church has to an official statement on the appropriate architecture for prayer book worship is *The Church for Common Prayer* (1994), published by the Episcopal Church Building Fund. It lays out a solid rationale for the reordering of worship spaces in light of the theology of the prayer book.

Several ecumenical and Roman Catholic resources offer reflections on the architectural setting for worship that are consistent with the implications of *The Book of Common Prayer: Environment and Art in Catholic Worship* is an official statement from the Roman Catholic Bishops' Committee on the Liturgy and is available from Liturgy Training Publications; *Shaping a House for the Church* by Marchita Mauck (Chicago: Liturgy Training Publications, 1990) includes many drawings and photographs, as does *A Place for Baptism* by Regina Kuehn (Chicago: Liturgy Training Publications, 1992). A classic resource for contemporary church architecture is Edward A. Sövik's *Architecture for Worship* (Minneapolis: Augsburg Publishing, 1973) and the chapter in James F. White's *Introduction to Christian Worship* (Nashville: Abingdon, 1981) on "The Language of Space" is a fine introduction to the topic written by a Methodist with deep ecumenical sensitivity.

～ Expansive Language

A searching exploration of the task of finding language for God that takes feminist perspectives into account is *She Who Is: The Mystery of God in Feminist Theological Discourse* by Elizabeth A. Johnson (New York: Crossroads, 1993). A very readable introduction to questions of how language affects believing and praying is James E. Griffiss' *Naming the Mystery* (Cambridge, Mass.: Cowley Publications, 1990—out of print). I would also recommend the introduction to *Enriching Our Worship* (New York: Church Publishing,

1997), and the chapter titled "Expansive Language, a Matter of Justice" by William Seth Adams in *A Prayer Book for the 21st Century,* Liturgical Studies Three (New York: Church Hymnal, 1996).

~ Devotional Reading

In *Prayer Book Spirituality* (New York: Church Hymnal, 1989), editor J. Robert Wright organizes a rich array of classic Anglican sources according to major sections of the prayer book. This is a source for reading something of what Richard Hooker had to say about the eucharist or George Herbert's reflections on common prayer—a wonderful view into classic Anglican piety as shaped by the prayer book. Liturgy Training Publications produces a series of books known as "Sourcebooks." These are collections of ancient and modern texts—liturgical texts, poetry, bits of essays—having to do with the seasons and liturgies of the church. There are currently thirteen of them, from *An Advent Sourcebook* to *A Sourcebook for the Lord's Day.* They offer an astonishing array of reflective material about worship.

~ The Future of Prayer Book Revision

Two important works on the future of the American prayer book have been published recently by Church Publishing. *A Prayer Book for the 21st Century* (1996) is a collection of essays aimed at "expanding the conversation" regarding issues for future prayer book revision—the essays address issues in each major section of the prayer book. Ruth A. Meyers's *Continuing the Reformation: Re-Visioning Baptism in the Episcopal Church* (1997) is a thorough historical and theological study of the development of the understanding and practice of baptism in the Episcopal Church and the implications of that development for the future self-understanding of the church.

⌒ Audiovisual Resources

A beautiful meditation on the eucharist without any words except those of the liturgy itself is the video "Do this in Remembrance of Me," available from the Episcopal Media Center (800/229-3788 or http://www.episcopalmediacenter.org).

The Episcopal Media Center also has audio tapes on liturgical topics, including several with examples and instructions on singing the liturgy. The daily office is sung by the brothers of the Society of St. John the Evangelist on several recordings available from Cowley Publications.

The Episcopal Church Building Fund has a video-tape titled "Churches for Common Prayer" showcasing ways in which both new and renovated church buildings can be responsive to the rites of *The Book of Common Prayer.* And a moving video presentation of the Easter Vigil with a baptism of adult catechumens is presented in "This is the Night" from Liturgy Training Publications.

Increasingly the Internet is providing resources and forums for liturgical ministry. A good place to start exploring this resource is the webpage of Anglicans Online (http://www.anglican.org/online/), where there are many links to liturgical resources on the web.

Questions for Group Discussion

～ Chapter 1: What is Common Prayer?

1. This chapter addresses the question of what is common prayer. How would you describe the defining characteristics of common prayer? What would "uncommon" prayer look like?

2. Jeffrey Lee describes Anglicans as "people of a book." Do you agree with this description? What are some of the advantages of having a prayer book? What are some of the disadvantages?

3. Lee asserts that "one of the challenges facing Anglicanism world-wide is the increasing diversity of its prayer books." How do you think the recent abundance of prayer book revisions have affected your congregation? Your own faith?

～ Chapter 2: The Pattern of Prayer

1. Why might it be important to worship in ways that are "older than what the pastor thought up last week"?

2. Read again the passages from Justin Martyr and Hippolytus quoted on pages 28 and 29 concerning the celebration of the eucharist in the early church. What similarities and differences do you see in the way we celebrate the eucharist today?

3. How have baptisms today changed from the way baptisms were done in the early church? What effect do you think the changes have had on the church in general? on your life as a Christian?

～ Chapter 3: The Prayer Book is Born

1. In what different settings have you worshiped? How did the place of worship affect the way you prayed?

2. Lee notes that "worship according to a single prayer book was to be the distinguishing feature of church life in England," rather than adherence to a particular set of doctrines. Do you think that is still true of Anglicanism today? What might be some of the strengths of that stance? Weaknesses?

3. According to Lee, the prayer book tradition "seeks to honor the church's tradition while engaging newly emerging realities of the present." How do you think the 1979 *Book of Common Prayer* reflects the experience of Anglicans today?

∼ Chapter 4: The American Prayer Book

1. Why do you think almost all revisions of the prayer book have elicited deep negative reactions that oppose change?

2. According to Lee, the nineteenth century was a time of tremendous change in the worship of the Episcopal Church. What elements brought in during that time are important to your worship today? Why?

3. As Episcopalians begin to contemplate another revision of the prayer book, what do you think we have learned from our experience of revising the 1928 *Book of Common Prayer?*

∼ Chapter 5: A Baptismal Church

1. Read the *Exultet* from the liturgy for the Easter Vigil (BCP 286–287). In what ways does this ancient song reflect the beliefs and identity of the church today?

2. Turn in the prayer book to the Additional Directions for Holy Baptism (BCP 312–314). Do they reflect your experience of baptism? Do you have questions about some of them? Which directions surprise you? Why?

3. In the same way that the baptism in *Life with Father* exemplified the Episcopal Church almost one hundred years ago, what do you think the way we do baptisms tells us about who we are as a church at the turn of this century?

∾ Chapter 6: The Eucharist and Daily Office

1. Turn in the prayer book to An Order for Celebrating the Holy Eucharist (BCP 400–401). If you were responsible for planning a service for a prayer group that met regularly in your home, what elements would you include in each section? Why? In other words, how would you "flesh out" the outline provided here to meet the needs of your particular group?

2. An outline for intercessory prayer in the eucharist is provided at the top of page 383 in the prayer book. Using any or all of the six forms that follow as models, craft a set of intercessions that could be used in your congregation during the eucharist next Sunday.

3. Which of the six eucharistic prayers in the prayer book do you find the most meaningful? Why? Which do you like the least? Why?

∾ Chapter 7: Liturgy in Action

1. In this chapter Lee notes that "many people live today in a state of ritual impoverishment." What family or social rituals can you remember keeping as a child? What rituals do you keep in your extended family or community today? How have they changed over time?

2. Think about the way you have experienced the sacraments, both now and in the past. How have the liturgical "fundamentals" Lee describes—the bread and wine of the eucharist, the water and oil of baptism, the orders of ministry, the liturgical year, the font,

table, scriptures, and music—shaped your experience of grace?

3. Have you participated in the planning of a church liturgy before? If so, what resources did you use? If you were in the shoes of the senior warden in charge of planning a service of evening prayer, what would you do?

∼ **Chapter 8: Looking Toward the Future**
1. Lee states that developing multicultural liturgies involves "trusting that the patterns of Christian worship will find faithful new expression in the communities that come to own them." What might an Anglican liturgy expressed through various cultures look like in your city or community? In your congregation? What experience have you had of liturgical celebrations in cultures other than your own?

2. How would you describe the "ordered freedom" provided by the prayer book? What boundaries of the prayer book tradition are most important to you? Why?

3. What thoughts and feelings do you have when you hear leaders in the church raise the possibility of revising the prayer book you currently use? What revisions do you think are needed? What would you add? change? remove? In what form(s) would you publish the new prayer book?

Cowley Publications is a ministry of the Society of St. John the Evangelist, a religious community for men in the Episcopal Church. Emerging from the Society's tradition of prayer, theological reflection, and diversity of mission, the press is centered in the rich heritage of the Anglican Communion.

Cowley Publications seeks to provide books, audio cassettes, and other resources for the ongoing theological exploration and spiritual development of the Episcopal Church and others in the body of Christ. To this end, it is dedicated to developing a new generation of theological writers, encouraging them to produce timely, creative, and stimulating publications of excellence, and making these publications available widely, reaching both clergy and lay persons.